Wild Cards

THE **ST. LOUIS CARDINALS'** STUNNING 2011 CHAMPIONSHIP SEASON

Rob Rains

TRIUMPH
BOOKS

TRIUMPHBOOKS**.COM**

This book is available in quantity at special discounts for your group or organization.
For further information, contact:

Triumph Books LLC
542 South Dearborn Street
Suite 750
Chicago, Illinois 60605
(312) 939–3330
Fax (312) 663–3557

www.triumphbooks.com

Printed in U.S.A.
ISBN: 978-1-60078-717-1

Content packaged by Mojo Media, Inc.
Joe Funk: Editor
Jason Hinman: Creative Director
Daniel Tideman: Art Director

Interior photos courtesy of AP Images

Contents

Introduction

The last thing anybody on the Cardinals wanted to do on the night of August 24 was attend the Knights of the Cauliflower Ear dinner, an annual event sponsored by a group of St. Louis businessmen.

That afternoon the Dodgers had completed a three-game sweep of the Cardinals at Busch Stadium, dropping the team 10½ games out of a playoff spot with 32 games left in the season.

General Manager John Mozeliak got up to speak, and basically apologized to the 200 people in attendance that the season had not gone better. Then it was manager Tony La Russa's turn, and his speech basically boiled down to three words: "We won't quit."

Pitcher Adam Wainwright, whose season-ending injury in spring training had led most observers to predict the Cardinals' year had ended before it even began, took it one step further.

"We're still in this thing," Wainwright told the audience.

Not many people really believed that. This dinner happened to coincide with a players-only meeting, called to basically challenge the team.

"There were a few of us that felt something needed to be said," Carpenter said. "We needed to start playing like the St. Louis Cardinals play baseball. It was about not embarrassing ourselves. It was about continuing to play hard, to give something to our fans, no matter if we won or didn't win. It was just 'let's go play and have some fun.'"

Nobody, not even the most optimistic player or fan, could have predicted the run that began the following day when the Cardinals beat the Pirates: a run that allowed them to catch the Braves and make the playoffs on the final day of the season; a run that saw them upset the Phillies in the Division Series; a run that included an NL-pennant-winning victory over the Brewers; a run that ended with a scintillating seven-game World Series victory over the Texas Rangers, earning the 11th title in franchise history.

"This year was improbable, incredible, overwhelming," La Russa said. "Think about what we did."

"We kind of just said 'we've got to step it up,'" said third baseman David Freese, who went on to win MVP honors in both the NLCS and the World Series. "No matter how this ends, we've got to play to our talent, to our ability. I think when we played Atlanta, we were down 3–1 Friday night [September 9], first game. And [Craig] Kimbrel was pitching. Albert [Pujols] came in and got a screamer down the line and two runs scored and that changed our season. If we don't win that night, I think maybe things are different.

"I think we believed. That's what you've got to do in this game. We've got a group of guys with some talent, desire, and just a ton of heart. We kept plugging, we kept plugging. It's kind of surreal, but we've been rewarded."

Tony LaRussa proudly hoists the World Series trophy for all Cardinals fans to see.

World Series

Game 1: Cardinals 3, Rangers 2

In Game 1 of the 2011 World Series, Tony La Russa's parade of relievers began in the seventh inning, one coming in after another to each make the first World Series appearance of his career. Undoubtedly, it was an emotional moment for all of them, and they kept up their amazing performance from the National League Championship Series: the five relievers combined to record the last nine outs and preserve a 3–2 victory for the Cardinals over Texas.

And as much as this night meant to Fernando Salas, Marc Rzepczynski, and Jason Motte, it meant a little more for the two veterans of the group, Arthur Rhodes and Octavio Dotel.

Rhodes had been pitching in the major leagues since August 21, 1991, when he pitched four innings for Baltimore in a start against the Rangers. He was two months shy of his 22nd birthday. Little did Rhodes know

on that day that he would have to make 899 additional appearances, and pitch for more than 20 years, before his first World Series moment would finally arrive.

There was a time when Rhodes, who turned 42 on October 24 in the middle of the Series, thought the moment might never come. He almost retired a few years ago, but decided to keep pitching as a way to honor the memory of his son, Jordan, who died in December 2008 from an undisclosed illness when he was only five years old.

As he has done every time he has taken the mound since then, before Rhodes started pitching to Josh Hamilton with two outs in the eighth, he bent down and scratched the initials "J.R." into the dirt.

"As soon as I first stepped on that rubber I was in shock," Rhodes said. "Now that I've got that first game out of the way I'm ready to go in the next game. This moment was great. I give it to my little boy. Going out there my first game, the first pitch of the game was all for him. The World Series is all

Relief pitcher Arthur Rhodes fires home during the eighth inning of Game 1 of the World Series.

for him. When I'm on the mound he's there with me. I'm going to enjoy myself and he's going to enjoy himself. I know he's watching over me right now."

After taking a deep breath, Rhodes began to pitch, quickly falling behind Hamilton 2–0. He worked the count to 3–2 before Rhodes got him to fly out to center.

"I didn't have an easy hitter, I had a hard hitter," Rhodes said. "I had to stay calm and cool against that guy because he can hurt you with one swing."

Rhodes had relieved Dotel, who had waited only a dozen years before he made his first World Series outing a success. He retired both hitters he faced, Ian Kinsler and Elvis Andrus, in the eighth before giving way to the left-handed Rhodes to battle the left-handed-hitting Hamilton.

Dotel had to try to keep himself from getting too excited about finally making it into the World Series.

"I don't want to think about that because if I do I will put too much pressure on myself," Dotel said. "This is the World Series, but I don't want to think about that at that moment. After the season I will freak out—not now, because St. Louis needs me. It's very exciting, but it's hard for me to explain to you guys how I feel."

Motte thinks he knows.

"That was awesome for those guys," Motte said. "I've learned so much from them in the short time they've been here. Guys like that show you how you need to be on the mound. It's their first World Series, too, and they are probably just as excited as everyone else. They had a job to do and they went out there and did it. They didn't try to do more than they've been doing. What I love about this game is what I've learned from guys like that."

Both Dotel and Rhodes followed Rzepczynski to the mound. He had replaced Salas in the seventh with runners on first and second and one out, the runners having reached on a single and a walk. Rzepczynski ended the threat by striking out pinch-hitters Craig Gentry and Esteban German.

The work of the first four relievers set the stage for Motte, who once again retired all three batters he faced—Michael Young, Adrian Beltre, and Nelson Cruz—in the ninth. That extended his string of consecutive postseason outs to 22, dating back to game three of the Division Series against the Phillies.

The work of the bullpen made Allen Craig's pinch-hit RBI single in the sixth, which scored David Freese after his one-out double, stand up as the winning run. It was the first go-ahead RBI by a pinch-hitter in the sixth inning or later of a World Series game since 1996 and was the first by a Cardinal pinch-hitter since Brian Harper's short-lived go-ahead RBI in Game 6 of the 1985 World Series against Kansas City.

Mike Napoli's two-run homer for Texas off starter Chris Carpenter in the fifth had tied the game, wiping out the lead the Cardinals had taken in the fourth on a two-run single by Lance Berkman. Craig, batting for Carpenter, was able to give the bullpen the lead it needed, and they took over from there.

It likely has been the leadership of Rhodes and Dotel that has helped the Cardinals bullpen become so dominant in the postseason. They were there Wednesday night as well, providing that steady hand well before the relievers were called into the game.

"We understand we are in the World Series, but we try to keep everybody relaxed and not think about it, and not put too much pressure on ourselves," Dotel said. "If you make pitches you have a chance to win the game, and that's what we're trying to do. We have guys really doing their job and making pitches." ●

Albert Pujols celebrates as Matt Holliday comes into score behind him on Lance Berkman's RBI single in the fourth inning.

World Series
Game 2: Rangers 2, Cardinals 1

For most of the 2011 postseason, every move that Tony La Russa made turned out well. For eight innings of Game 2 at Busch Stadium, it looked as if that would be the case again.

Allen Craig's pinch-hit single—his second in two nights off Alexi Ogando—had broken a scoreless tie in the seventh inning. Fernando Salas and Marc Rzepcynski had protected the lead in the eighth, and La Russa turned the ball over to Jason Motte to get the three outs in the ninth that would send the Cardinals to Texas with a 2–0 lead in the World Series.

For the first time in the postseason, however, Motte was not perfect. He allowed a flare single to left to lead-off hitter Ian Kinsler, snapping a string of 25 consecutive batters Motte had retired dating back to Game 3 of the Division Series.

After Kinsler stole second, Elvis Andrus followed with another single; Kinsler was held up at third base. When the throw home from Jon Jay kicked off the glove of Albert Pujols, with an error charged to Pujols, Andrus was able to take second.

Josh Hamilton was coming to the plate. Now it was decision time for La Russa.

He could have walked Hamilton, which would have loaded the bases, and had Motte try to retire Michael Young. Or he could have left Motte in to pitch to Hamilton, who has been bothered all of the postseason by a groin injury.

Or La Russa could have done what he did, pull Motte and bring in Arthur Rhodes from the bullpen for the lefty-versus-lefty match-up. In virtually the same situation on Wednesday night—except that there were no runners on base—Hamilton had flied out against Rhodes.

On this night, Hamilton hit the first pitch from Rhodes for another fly ball, to right, deep enough to score Kinsler with the tying run and for Andrus to tag from second and move to third. Lance Lynn then relieved Rhodes, and he also got Young to hit a

David Freese celebrates after scoring the game's first run on a single by Allen Craig in the seventh inning.

fly ball, but it was deep enough for Andrus to score the run that gave the Rangers the 2–1 victory.

La Russa did not second-guess his decisions in the ninth inning, which proved that unless the players execute his game plan to perfection, the manager is only as good as his players. La Russa said he was reluctant to walk Hamilton because it would have loaded the bases with nobody out.

"That's a really difficult thing to do," he said. "We thought we had a chance to do something with Hamilton with Rhodes. Maybe they score a run but not advance the other guy. He did a good job. Young did a very good job of getting the ball to the outfield.

"I don't think walking him there would have made it easier for us. I think it maybe would have made it tougher. We did the best we could, they just did it better."

When asked if he thought about leaving Motte in to pitch to Hamilton, La Russa also said he didn't think that would have been a good idea either.

"From what I understand Hamilton handles a fastball pretty well," La Russa said. "If he (Andrus) had not gotten to second base we probably would have left Motte in there. But if you're thinking about how you can get an out and maybe not have the guy go from second to third, I thought the left-hander had a better chance. He did good, he got an out, it was just a really good piece of hitting."

Said Rhodes: "I knew he was going to swing at the first pitch no matter what. He just hit it deep enough to get the run home and that was it."

It has been Motte who has been on the other end of most of these kinds of games for the Cardinals lately, but he was willing to accept the blame on a night when the outcome did not go his team's way.

"I didn't do my job tonight," Motte said. "You just have to learn from what you do on the bad days and come back out. This isn't the first time we've lost a game. I blame myself because I just went out there and didn't make my pitches."

It looked as if the Cardinals might have a chance to mount a comeback of their own in the bottom of the ninth when Yadier Molina drew a leadoff walk from Neftali Feliz. Nick Punto fouled off two bunt attempts, however, then struck out. Schumaker also struck out before Feliz got the final out by retiring Rafael Furcal on a fly ball to right.

This was the first time a team had trailed going into the ninth inning of a World Series game and rallied to win since Arizona did it in Game 7 of the 2001 Series against the Yankees. This night was also the first time in World Series history that both the tying and go-ahead runs were driven in by sacrifice flies.

It also was the first time the Cardinals had led a World Series game 1–0 going into the ninth inning since Game 6 in 1985 against the Royals. That game, thanks to Don Denkinger and Dane Iorg's two-run single, also turned out to be a St. Louis defeat. The Cardinals have never played a World Series game that ended 1–0.

The loss spoiled an outstanding performance from Cardinals' starter Jaime Garcia, who shut out the Rangers on three hits through the seventh, before he was lifted for the pinch-hitter Craig. Garcia walked one and struck out seven in his best start of the postseason.

"That's a major step that he can rely on the rest of his career," La Russa said. "He's done that for us a bunch of times his first two years. But you could have considered this situation and these circumstances, that's huge for us and for him."

The loss meant that for the first time in more than two months the Cardinals would not have a "happy flight," as they traveled to Texas and the next three games of the series. The last time they had lost a game on a "getaway day" was August 3, a streak of 17 consecutive wins. ●

Jaime Garcia had an excellent outing in Game 2, but the Cardinals still came up short.

World Series
Game 3: Cardinals 16, Rangers 7

What happened in Game 3 really should not have come as a surprise. There have been way too many occasions in the past 11 years where something upset Albert Pujols and he ended up delivering a resounding response with his bat.

It happened again, and this time the result might have been one of the single greatest performances in baseball history.

Over a two-day period, Pujols had been the focus of several negative stories in the national media after he failed to talk to reporters following Game 2. Pujols had committed an error during the Rangers' ninth-inning rally in that game. The stories attacked his credentials as a team leader. They criticized him for a lack of responsibility and said he had displayed a lack of accountability, leaving it to the team's younger players to address the reasons for the Cardinals' 2–1 loss to Texas.

There were suggestions that the Cardinals had two sets of rules for their players, one for Pujols and one for everybody else.

After a day of trying to defuse the controversy as the World Series shifted to Texas, Pujols decided to answer his critics the best way he knows how—

with his bat. And when a player can do what Pujols did on this night, powering the Cardinals to a 16–7 victory, there is one rule that will never change in baseball: that player gets to set the rules and do whatever he wants.

Pujols hit three homers, becoming only the third player in history to do that in a World Series game, joining Reggie Jackson, who did it in 1977 and Babe Ruth, who did it twice, in 1926 and 1928, both times against the Cardinals.

He became the second player in World Series history to record five hits in a game, joining Paul Molitor of the Brewers in 1982, who did it against the Cardinals.

He became only the third player in World Series history to drive in six runs in a game. The other two were Bobby Richardson in 1960 and Hideki Matsui in 2009.

He became the first player in World Series history to record 14 total bases in a game, breaking the old mark of 12 set by Ruth and tied by Jackson.

He also became the first person in history to accomplish all of that in the same game.

"I saw him on TV," said Texas manager Ron Washington, "but I'll tell you, tonight was something special."

That might qualify for the understatement of the year.

Albert Pujols belts the first of his three homers, a titanic three-run shot in the sixth inning.

Pujols said after the game that he actually was embarrassed about the media controversy that arose after Game 2, but it did not affect his goal of what he wanted to do in this game.

"Not really," Pujols said. "What can I say? To tell you the truth, I just come and get ready to play. I've been in that situation before where people just blow things out, and it is what it is, and you can't really think about that. My main focus is we are in the World Series.

"I feel embarrassed that everybody was just focused on that, and I was in the middle of that, when you had Jaime (Garcia) out there throwing one of his best postseason games ever and you had (Colby) Lewis doing the same thing against some tough offense. I was really embarrassed, to tell you the truth, that we were in the middle of that."

Nobody will be talking about anything in this game except Pujols' record-breaking performance. Forgotten will be Craig's first-inning homer, which meant the Cardinals scored first in their 10th consecutive game, a postseason record. Gone will be the mini-controversy about a disputed call by first-base umpire Ron Kulpa, and David Freese extending his postseason hitting streak to 13 consecutive games will be an afterthought.

People won't even be talking about Yadier Molina's four-RBI night, or the fact the Cardinals set a franchise record for a World Series game by scoring 16 runs, three more than they scored in Game 6 of the 1982 World Series.

World Series games quickly are given labels. Reggie Jackson became Mr. October the night he hit the three home runs in 1977 to win the championship for the Yankees. Game 3 in Milwaukee in 1982 became known to Cardinal fans as the Willie McGee game. Game 6 in 1985 will forever be known as the Don Denkinger game,

And what happened on this night will go through the ages as Albert's game, the night he once again showed the world that he is without a doubt the best player in the game.

Pujols did not even seem all that excited after the night was over. Reporters kept trying to get him to open up and discuss how it felt to experience a night like this during his postgame news conference, and he would not get drawn into that conversation.

"To tell you the truth, I won't lie, I don't concentrate on numbers," Pujols said. "I just said it, this is not an individual game; this is a team effort. That's what I try to do every day, to go out there and help my ballclub to win however I can. Hopefully at the end of my career I can look back and say, wow, what a game it was in Game 3 in 2011, but as of

right now, it's great to get this win and just move on pretty much and get ready to play tomorrow."

The Rangers actually retired Pujols on a ground ball in the first inning, making him 0-for-7 in the series at that point. He singled during the Cardinals' four-run fourth but was retired on a fielder's choice grounder by Matt Holliday. He had a leadoff single in the three-run fifth. It turned out he was saving all of his dramatic moments for later in the game.

After Ogando finally retired Craig for the first time in the series in the sixth, Pujols unloaded a three-run bomb that hit off the second-deck façade in left field. Batting again in the seventh, he hit a two-run blast into the seats in left center, becoming the first Cardinal to hit two home runs in a World Series game since McGee's game in 1982. The homer also made him the first player in World Series history to get a hit in four consecutive innings in a game.

He was the third scheduled hitter in the ninth inning, and with the Cardinals ahead by nine runs, he turned to La Russa in the dugout and asked if the manager wanted to get backup catcher Gerald Laird an at-bat in his place.

"Tony said he wasn't going to take me out of the game," Pujols said.

So Pujols delivered his third homer of the game, off a third pitcher. It was the fifth time in his career he has hit three homers in a game, the other four times coming during the regular season.

"There was a couple times in that dugout about the middle of the game somebody kept saying, 'he's having a day he'll never forget,'" La Russa said. "And that's kind of what he did."

La Russa has been Pujols' manager ever since he was a rookie in 2001, which makes him qualified to answer the question of where this game will rank among Pujols' Hall of Fame accomplishments.

"According to some of the stats, it's the greatest of any World Series in 120 years," La Russa said. "Fourteen total bases and the five hits, four innings in a row and five hits.... I think the best thing to do is you make that statement and ask somebody, 'okay, show me one that was better.' I think it would be hard to do.

"I'll tell you, and it's a real good P.S. to this, and I've learned it over 11 years with Albert, he will probably think about this and enjoy it, and he should. If you see him tomorrow, you would never, ever suspect that he did this tonight. He will be into his routine, getting ready. He is so strong in his mind, and we'll see. I know (Derek) Holland has got real good stuff, but Albert will go about it in a way that is why—that's part of his greatness."

Yadier Molina, who had a good game himself, congratulates Albert Pujols after Pujols' historic Game 3 performance.

Albert Pujols

Joins elite company with three-homer game

Albert Pujols joined a pretty select group of company when he hit three home runs in the third game of the 2011 World Series against Texas. The only two players who had accomplished that feat previously were New York Yankees legends Babe Ruth and Reggie Jackson.

Ruth did it twice, in 1926 and again in 1928. Both games came against the Cardinals. Jackson's feat came in Game 6 of the 1977 Series against the Dodgers. His performance helped earn him the nickname "Mr. October."

Jackson was listening to Game 3 on the radio after running a quick errand near his home in Carmel, California, as Pujols came to bat in the ninth inning against the Rangers. The Cardinals' slugger had already hit two home runs.

"I thought, if this guy hits one, it would be pretty awesome," Jackson said.

Speaking about the accomplishment the next day in a phone interview with the St. Louis Post-Dispatch, Jackson said, "It truly is an honor for me. It makes it a little more special for me. Nobody understands how great Ruth was. It was too long ago, a different game. Ruth hit more homers than most teams.

"This makes it relative for today's fan. When it's Pujols, who is the undisputed best in the game, it shows how special it is."

Jackson and Pujols talked on the telephone a day after Pujols' three-homer game, a discussion Jackson described as one of mutual admiration. The two had met each other in the past, and had an extended conversation at the 2007 All-Star game in Detroit.

Jackson's three home runs came in the championship-clinching game for the Yankees, helping New York to an 8–4 victory. They capped a series in which he hit five home runs, scored 10 runs, had 25 bases and led all hitters with a .450 average. He homered in the fourth inning off the Dodgers' Burt Hooton, in the fifth off Elias Sosa, and in the eighth off Charlie Hough in the game at Yankee Stadium.

Ruth's first three-homer game came in the fourth game of the 1926 Series at Sportsman's Park in St. Louis, a game the Yankees won 10–5. He hit his first two homers off Flint Rehm, in the first and third inning, and his final blast came in the sixth off Hi Bell.

One of the homers reportedly was hit out of the ballpark, across Grand Street, and broke a window at the Wells Chevrolet dealership.

Ruth also became famous in the 1926 World Series for making the final out, when he was thrown out trying to steal second in the ninth inning of Game 7.

Two years later, Ruth hit .625 in the World Series and had his second three-homer game, also at Sportsman's Park, in the fourth game against the Cardinals. He homered off Bill Sherdel in the fourth and seventh innings, and then connected again off Pete Alexander in the eighth. The 7–3 win clinched a sweep by the Yankees. ●

Albert Pujols watches as his historic third home run of Game 3 puts him in the record books next to Reggie Jackson and Babe Ruth.

World Series

Game 4: Rangers 4, Cardinals 0

Edwin Jackson was philosophical after he suffered the loss for the Cardinals in the fourth game of the 2011 World Series, knowing he could have pitched better but also knowing the result could have been much worse.

Struggling with his control all night, Jackson managed to pitch around five walks and three hits through the first five innings of the game, allowing the Rangers to score only one run.

"My mantra was to just keep the game close regardless of how it was, whether it looked pretty or not," Jackson said. "Just try to keep the game within striking distance, especially at this park."

Jackson knew, however, that he could not continue to walk people or it would catch up with him, and that finally happened in the sixth.

After he issued one-out walks to Nelson Cruz and David Murphy—each time after getting two strikes—Jackson

came out of the game. Reliever Mitchell Boggs left a fastball up over the plate on his first pitch to Mike Napoli, who slammed a three-run homer into the seats in left field.

"Some pitches were close, some weren't," Jackson said. "When you're over the plate you can't always expect to get close pitches. At the end of the day you have to make them put the ball in play. You don't want to walk seven guys, but I managed to battle through it and get out of situations. It's just a matter of time before it catches up to you."

The seven walks tied the Cardinal franchise record for most walks in a World Series game, set by Bill Hallahan in 1931. It also was the most walks in a Series game since Florida's Livan Hernandez walked eight in Game 5 in 1997 against the Indians. The seven walks also were the most in a game by Jackson since he walked eight while pitching a no-hitter for Arizona against Tampa Bay in 2010.

Pitching coach Dave Duncan thought the result could have been dif-

As this photo of Lance Berkman arguing with the umpire after striking out reveals, the Game 4 loss was frustrating for the Cardinals.

ferent if some of Jackson's pitches had been called strikes by home plate umpire Ron Kulpa.

"I don't think he would have walked seven if he had got as many borderline pitches called strikes as the other team did. We didn't get any borderline pitches called," Duncan said. "With that club you've got to pitch on the edges. You can't pitch in the middle of the plate. That's what we were trying to do all night and that's probably why he walked seven guys."

While Jackson was getting into and out of jams, the Cardinals offense had no answers for Texas starter Derek Holland. A night after St. Louis scored 16 runs, Holland shut them out for 8⅓ innings, falling two outs shy of throwing the first shutout by an AL pitcher since Jack Morris won Game 7 of the 1991 Series.

Manager Ron Washington took out Holland, who allowed only two hits, after he walked Rafael Furcal with one out in the ninth. Neftali Feliz relieved and after walking Jon Jay retired Albert Pujols and Matt Holliday to end the game and tie up the Series at two wins each.

The last AL pitcher to throw 8⅓ shutout innings in a World Series was Andy Petitte of the Yankees in 1996.

Lance Berkman had both St. Louis hits, a double in the second and a single in the fifth. After the latter hit, he was quickly erased in a double play. Albert Pujols was 0-for-4 one night after he got five hits and three homers.

"You've got to give credit to Holland," said third baseman David Freese, whose postseason hitting streak was snapped at 13 games. "He was impressive. You don't want to give too much credit to an opposing pitcher, but he was fantastic."

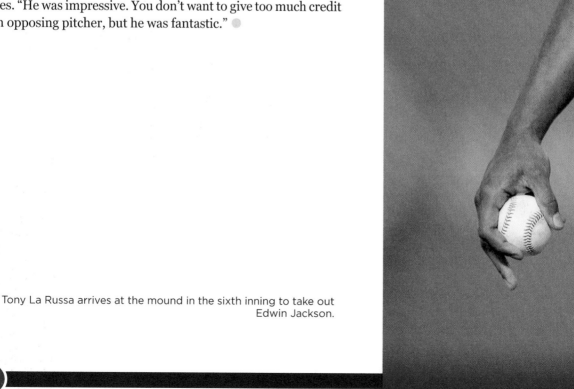

Tony La Russa arrives at the mound in the sixth inning to take out Edwin Jackson.

World Series

Game 5: Rangers 4, Cardinals 2

A botched telephone conversation between the Cardinals' dugout and bullpen might have cost the team a chance to win Game 5.

With the 2011 World Series knotted at two wins each, the Rangers batting in the eighth inning, and the score tied 2–2, manager Tony La Russa twice called the bullpen from the dugout phone wanting Jason Motte to get up and start throwing.

Neither time did bullpen coach Derek Lilliquist hear or understand La Russa's request. That set off a disastrous chain of events that ended up with Mike Napoli hitting a two-run double off Marc Rzepczynski, and the Rangers won the game 4–2. The victory put the Rangers one win away from the first world championship in the franchise's 51-year history as the Series moved back to St. Louis for Game 6.

La Russa tried to explain what happened during the bizarre eighth inning when he met with the media after the game.

Octavio Dotel had relieved Chris Carpenter to start the inning, and when La Russa called down to the bullpen, he wanted Rzepczynski and Motte to get up and begin throwing. Lilliquist never heard Motte's name. When La Russa realized that Motte was not warming up, he made a second phone call and asked again for Motte to get up. This time the coach thought La Russa was asking for Lance Lynn to start throwing.

After Michael Young opened the inning by getting a double off Dotel, the reliever struck out Adrian Beltre, whose home run off Carpenter in the sixth had tied the game. Instead of letting Dotel pitch to the right-handed Nelson Cruz, La Russa ordered an intentional walk, which he hoped would set up a potential double play.

La Russa went to the mound and brought in Rzepczynski to pitch to the left-handed David Murphy, hoping to get a ground ball. He did, but it deflected off Rzepczynski's knee and second baseman Nick Punto was

Nick Punto's bat made it all the way to first base with him as he flied out in the second inning.

unable to make a play on the ball, loading the bases.

That was when La Russa learned that Motte had never gotten up and started throwing, so he was not ready to come into the game.

"I was thinking that we had a real good chance with Rzepczynski to get an out, and then we were going to pitch around Napoli and go after the left-hander, Moreland," La Russa said. "If that doesn't happen then Motte was supposed to be ready for Napoli."

But because the bullpen had never heard the instruction to get Motte up, La Russa had no choice but to leave Rzepczynski in to face Napoli, who is a much more dangerous hitter against left-handers. On a 1–1 pitch he came through with the two-run double.

The inning became even more bizarre, if possible, after Rzepczynski struck out Moreland. La Russa went to the mound and signaled for the right-hander, expecting Motte, but was surprised when Lynn came trotting in instead.

"Why are you here?" La Russa asked, knowing Lynn was supposed to be used in this game only in the case of an emergency.

So, not wanting to have Lynn pitch in the game, he had him intentionally walk Ian Kinsler, giving Motte time to finally warm up so he could come into the game. He did, striking out Elvis Andrus with the bases loaded to end the inning.

La Russa actually was very calm in explaining what happened, and appeared more frustrated and upset by all of the wasted opportunities the Cardinals had to add on to their early 2–0 lead.

The team continued an ugly trend in the World Series by going 1-for-12 with runners in scoring position, the one hit an RBI single by Yadier Molina that drove in the first St. Louis run in the second. They left the bases loaded twice and stranded a total of 12 runners. In the four games in the Series besides the 16-run outburst in Game 3, the Cardinals were only 4-for-30 with runners in scoring position.

Texas intentionally walked Albert Pujols three times in Game 5, including once with nobody on base, the first time that has ever happened in World Series history.

Cleanup hitter Matt Holliday followed the three intentional walks by hitting into a double play, striking out, and finally hitting a single to left, which ended an 0-for-6 streak in those situations in the postseason.

When he was not intentionally walked, Pujols was 0-for-2, making him 0-for-12 in the four games other than his monster three-homer performance in Game 3.

"We had a lot of chances," La Russa said. "It's a really tough loss. We had an opportunity to add on where we could have given ourselves some room for a slipup and still won the game. It's disappointing."

The problem with the botched communication between the dugout and bullpen was not the only mix-up of the night, either. In the seventh inning of the tie game, after Allen Craig had walked, he took off in an apparent attempt to steal second. Pujols apparently had put the hit-and-run sign on himself, but the pitch from Alexi Ogando was so high that Pujols did not swing, and Craig was thrown out easily at second.

La Russa would not say who was at fault on the play.

"It was a mix-up," La Russa said. On our team we don't throw anybody under the bus. It was a mix-up. That's all I'm going to say."

Craig again reached base in the ninth when he was hit by a pitch thrown by Neftali Feliz. When the count to Pujols went to 3–2, Craig took off again for second. Pujols swung and missed for strike three, and Craig again was thrown out by Napoli, who was a star with both his bat and his arm on this night. The two RBIs by Napoli gave him nine for the Series, compared to 10 for the rest of the Rangers.

The Cardinals had one final chance after the strike out-caught stealing double play. Holliday walked, but Berkman, representing the tying run, struck out to end the game. ●

Frustration for Tony La Russa as he waits for Jason Motte to finally enter the game in the eighth inning.

World Series

Game 6: Cardinals 10, Rangers 9 (11 innings)

Even though David Freese had played this moment out a million times before, in his childhood, in his dreams, the reality was far greater than anything he could have ever imagined.

A Cardinals fan ever since he could hold a baseball, growing up in suburban St. Louis, Freese twice stepped to the plate at Busch Stadium in Game 6 with the season on the line.

In the ninth inning, Freese came to bat with two outs and the Cardinals losing 7–5. Two runners were on base as the largest crowd in Busch Stadium III history stood as one, hoping this team that refused to die had one more comeback in them.

Texas closer Neftali Feliz worked the count to a ball and two strikes before Freese connected with the next pitch. The ball appeared headed for the right field seats, but fell a few feet short, bouncing off the Gulf sign on the wall. Both runners scored and Freese slid into third with a triple.

The game was tied and headed for the 10th. Josh Hamilton of the Rangers then became the hero of the moment with a two-run homer that put Texas back on top 9–7. Did the Cardinals have *another* comeback in them?

"We've been left for dead for months," Lance Berkman said, "but no time's bigger than tonight."

The Cardinals opened the 10th with singles by Daniel Descalso and Jon Jay. After pitcher Kyle Lohse sacrificed, Ryan Theriot's ground ball to third scored Descalso. Albert Pujols was intentionally walked, bringing Berkman up to bat.

The team's best hitter in this World Series was calm as he came to the plate. Not a very emotional player, Berkman said he knew he would either come through or be ready to go spend time with his family all winter.

"I figured I was in a no-lose situation," Berkman said.

Like Freese, he battled until he had two strikes. For the second time in two innings, the Cardinals were down to their last strike. And Berkman came through as well, lining a single to center that drove in the tying run.

"We were like Lazarus," Berkman said. "We came back from the dead."

The stadium was rocking as Jake Westbrook, the seventh Cardinals

Teammates celebrate with David Freese after he hit a walk-off home run in the 11th inning of Game 6 to give the Cardinals an incredible 10-9 win, tying the series 3-3.

pitcher, retired the Rangers in the top of the 11th. Freese led off the bottom of the inning against Mark Lowe hoping to start a game-winning rally.

Instead, he delivered one of the most dramatic home runs in Cardinals' history, sending a 3–2 pitch over the center field wall to give St. Louis a 10–9 victory, setting up the first Game 7 in the World Series since 2002.

As he called the game on Fox television, Joe Buck repeated the game-ending call of his father Jack 20 years earlier, when Kirby Puckett hit a walk-off homer for the Twins in Game 6 of the 1991 World Series.

"We'll see you tomorrow night," Buck said.

"When you are down to your last strike no one is ever thinking 'This is great,'" Berkman said. "But this is as great a game as I've ever played in. This was an ugly game for about six or seven innings, but then it got beautiful in a hurry."

How special was this game? Here are just a few of the reasons:

- The Cardinals became the first team in World Series history to come back twice from deficits of two runs in the ninth inning or later.
- The Cardinals became the first team to score in the eighth, ninth, and 10th innings of a World Series game.
- This was the 15th game to end on a walk-off home run in World Series history and was the fourth Game 6 to end on a walk-off homer, the first since Joe Carter's homer won the 1993 World Series for Toronto.
- It was the first time Freese had hit a walk-off home run in his life.
- It was the third postseason walk-off homer in Cardinals' history, but the first in the World Series. The others came in the NLCS, by Ozzie Smith in 1985 and Jim Edmonds in 2004.

Manager Tony La Russa admitted there were a couple of points late in the game where he was thinking about how the Cardinals were going to salute the fans, before the Rangers began celebrating the first world championship in the franchise's 51-year history.

"There were a couple of times in the ninth and 10th," La Russa said, "when I was forced to say, 'go down to the bullpen. We've got to do the fans right.' We went from that to celebrating."

Freese's teammates were having a hard time letting this moment sink in.

"This is something else," Pujols said. "Everybody who was here or watching on television is going to remember this game. If we can finish it up tomorrow it will become even sweeter."

Pujols was happiest for Freese, the St. Louis kid who delivered the first home run by a native since Mike Shannon's homer in Game 7 in the 1968 World Series.

"Nobody in this clubhouse has been through more stuff than him," Pujols said. "Nobody in here deserves it more than him."

Freese got the baseball he hit into history, trading an autographed bat and a World Series ball autographed by the team for it. His bat and the shredded jersey his teammates tore off his back as he arrived at home plate are headed for the Hall of Fame in Cooperstown.

And Freese knows the lasting legacy of what he did will be how many youngsters in the St. Louis area will become David Freese in their backyard games, and go to bed at night dreaming about becoming the next David Freese when they grow up, hitting a home run to win a World Series game for the Cardinals.

Freese doesn't have to dream about that anymore.

Matt Holliday and Rafael Furcal not only collide, but can't come up with a ball hit by Nelson Cruz in the fourth inning.

World Series
Game 7: Cardinals 6, Rangers 2

It was understandable that David Freese had a difficult time getting to sleep after his history-making home run in the sixth game of the 2011 World Series.

The reason Freese couldn't sleep, however, was because he was looking ahead—to Game 7—not looking back on what had just happened.

"I was so focused on this game," Freese said. "You roll on adrenaline this time of year."

Freese and the rest of the Cardinals had forced the 11th Game 7 in franchise history—the first since 1987—but they knew in their hearts that a loss in that game would severely tarnish what they had just accomplished.

The team that had refused to die for two months did so one more time, thanks in large measure to Freese.

The Rangers jumped on Chris Carpenter, starting on three days rest, for two runs in the top of the first inning, but Freese's two-run double following walks to Albert Pujols and Lance Berkman wiped out that early advantage.

It would be the only comeback the Cardinals would need on this night en route to the 11th world championship in franchise history. They also became the ninth team in a row to come home trailing three games to two in the Series and then win both Game 6 and Game 7 in their park.

Allen Craig, playing in place of the injured Matt Holliday, hit his third homer of the World Series in the third inning to put the Cardinals ahead to stay. It was the first homer by a Cardinal in Game 7 of the World Series since Mike Shannon hit one in 1968. Unlike most of the previous six games in this Series, there was little drama on this night, and that was perfectly okay with the Cardinals.

Both Freese and Craig made contributions with their gloves as well as their bats in handing the Rangers their first back-to-back losses since August 25—a string of 46 consecutive games. The loss gave Texas the unfortunate distinction of becoming the first team to lose the World Series in consecutive years since the Braves in 1991 and 1992.

Chris Carpenter took the mound in Game 7 and his unflappable performance helped propel the Cardinals to victory.

In the fifth inning, the Rangers had the tying run on second with one out when Freese made a lunging catch over the railing in front of the Texas dugout of a foul popup hit by Josh Hamilton. Carpenter then struck out Michael Young to end the inning, and really the last Texas threat.

"You've got to tip your hat to Carpenter," said Texas manager Ron Washington. "After that first inning we pressured him a little bit, but he bent, he didn't break. And they ended up putting some runs on the board and winning the ballgame."

Carpenter and four relievers retired 14 of the final 15 Texas batters, allowing only a ground rule double by David Murphy in the seventh. One of the outs came when a leaping Craig took a home run away from Nelson Cruz in the sixth, his glove reaching above the fence to make the catch.

"This is what you play for," Pujols said. "Standing at first base with three outs left, I was thinking about all of the things we went through this year as a group, just how special this group of guys is.... It's just an unbelievable feeling."

The two RBIs by Freese, the hometown kid, helped him capture the World Series MVP Award, following his earlier selection as MVP of the National League Championship Series. He finished the postseason with a record 21 RBIs and became the sixth player in history to be named the MVP of both series in the same season. The last position player to do it was the Cardinals' Darrell Porter in 1982.

"I'm trying to soak all of this in," Freese said. "I've tried to soak in this whole postseason as much as I can because you never know when it will be your last attempt at a title.

"I sit here right now, and I still can't believe that we actually did this. I keep thinking about the mood of the team in mid-August and the disappointment of what was going down. Carp said 'Let's get together and talk about some things.' Most importantly, we said that the fans deserve for us to make a run at this. They deserve this just as much as anybody else."

After getting out of the first inning, Carpenter gutted his way through six innings, becoming the first pitcher in postseason history to win two winner-take-all games, following his victory over Roy Halladay in a 1–0 complete game classic in Game 5 of the NLDS. He finished the year with a 4–0 postseason record.

"I didn't know how long they were going to let me go," Carpenter said. "So I was just trying to do everything I could to get one out at a time. I had no idea, and nobody said anything to me about it. I just continued to go out and try to make pitches. I was able to make some really good pitches when I had to."

The Cardinals added two insurance runs in the fifth, without a hit, bunching two walks, an intentional walk, and two hit batters. Molina's RBI single in the seventh further ensured the Cardinals and their fans would be celebrating deep into the night.

The final out of 2011 came when Jason Motte got Murphy to hit a fly ball to left. When the ball settled in Allen Craig's glove, the season—this incredible and unforgettable season—was over.

"This is what you dream about," said Tony La Russa, who earned his third World Championship ring. "Truly a dream come true. It's hard to really imagine it actually happened. It's hard to explain how we made it happen, except the club has great guts. Really we have more talent than people think, but we have great guts."

It was a win, and a season, that nobody involved will soon forget.

"Two months ago we were supposed to be watching the World Series," Albert Pujols observed after the game. "We went through a lot of tough times and a lot of sweet moments. Not too many teams do it like that."

Added Allen Craig, "This is an unbelievable group of guys. I wish everybody in the country could get to know these guys. I'm just glad to be a part of it." ●

Allen Craig reaches over the wall to catch a fly ball off the bat of Nelson Cruz and rob him of a home run in the sixth inning.

Regular Season

The ground crew works hard to finish field preparations before the first pitch against the San Diego Padres on Opening Day 2011.

Wainwright Lost

The Cardinals' challenges begin in spring training

Spring training is almost always a time for optimism. Even the major-league teams that realistically do not have a chance of contending for the pennant are hopeful as they arrive in Florida or Arizona, greeted by the warm, sunny skies, talking about how maybe this can be their year.

For teams that expect to be pennant-contenders, these days are the calm before the regular-season storm, the time to get in shape, work off the winter's rust and ensure that they are physically ready when Opening Day arrives.

That was all Adam Wainwright was trying to do as he walked to the mound on February 21, 2011, at the Cardinals spring training complex in Jupiter, Florida. It was his first time facing live hitters in camp. The right-handed ace of the team, Wainwright had won a combined 39 games the previous two seasons, the most in the majors. He saw no reason why 2011 should be any different.

A new diet and exercise plan had left him in the best physical shape of his career. He liked the new additions the Cardinals had made to the roster, particularly the signing of his close friend, Lance v, and he was as excited as he had ever been at this time of the year.

That all changed, however, when one pitch went terribly wrong that February day. He felt something pop in his right elbow, and he knew immediately all of that optimism he had for the 2011 season was gone. Tests and doctors evaluations over the next few days confirmed that he had torn a ligament in his pitching elbow and would have to undergo season-ending surgery.

After losing his season to injury, Adam Wainwright stuck with the team throughout 2011, though he was forced to wear this brace for several months as he recovered.

Not only did the injury alter Wainwright's plans for the season, it put a severe crimp on the Cardinals' hopes. Most observers immediately wrote off the team's chances of winning the World Series in 2011. The consensus opinion was that no team, no matter how much depth it had, could overcome the loss of a pitcher of Wainwright's stature.

Wainwright, while obviously disappointed with the injury, took a more optimistic approach to the news.

"Season over, no Cy Young, no competing, nothing," Wainwright said in his first public comments a few days later. "But, let me say this. I have learned more about myself in the last two days than in the last five years combined."

One of manager Tony La Russa's best traits is that he never lets himself or his team get down about an injury or another similar setback. He viewed the loss of Wainwright as an opportunity for another pitcher to step up and fill that gap, and that was the lesson he began preaching to his team.

By the end of the spring, as the Cardinals headed north to start the regular season, the loss of Wainwright was old news. All of the attention was now focused on the teams first baseman, and whether or not the 2011 season would be the final year in St. Louis for the three-time MVP, scheduled to become a free agent at the end of the year. •

Legendary Cardinals Bob Gibson and Bruce Sutter flank Adam Wainwright as they throw out ceremonial pitches before Game 1 of the World Series.

Opening Day

Potential free-agent Pujols faced unprecedented pressures

Whether he will ever admit it or not, Albert Pujols knew the 2011 baseball season would be different than any of the first 10 seasons of his spectacular career. Because he had a chance to become a free agent at the end of the season, virtually every game and every at-bat would be examined in almost microscopic detail.

Whether he will ever admit it or not, Albert Pujols knew the 2011 baseball season would be different than any of the first 10 seasons of his spectacular career. Because he had a chance to become a free agent at the end of the season, virtually every game and every at-bat would be examined in almost microscopic detail.

Pujols' accomplishments on the field no doubt would be the barometer fans used to measure how far the Cardinals should go to try to re-sign the second-best player in franchise history. Fans of other teams were watching as well, hoping that somehow Pujols would leave the Cardinals and sign with their team.

Pujols put himself in this situation by turning down the Cardinals' contract offer before spring training. His faith is strong enough that he was at peace with that decision, and he honestly believed that whatever happened after this year was what was meant to happen.

He received a rousing ovation from the fans at Busch Stadium before the March 31 game against San Diego, and noticed that the fans also cheered when former Cardinal Jim Edmonds threw out the first pitch and when ex-teammate Ryan Ludwick came to bat for the Padres.

What Pujols didn't hear, or read, were the comments from fans as he completed what arguably could have been the worst game of his Cardinals career.

This opening day was the 1,559[th] game of Pujols career and never had he done what he did against the Padres. He went 0-for-5, which he has done 28 times before, but he

An expectant Billy Ward looks on eagerly in the minutes before the first pitch of the 2011 season.

also grounded into three double plays. Pujols had never before grounded into more than two double plays in a game, something he has done eight times in 10 years.

"It was just a bad game, man," Pujols said afterward. "What, am I going to shoot myself up? Thats the way it goes. Its baseball."

La Russa thought Pujols hit the ball hard enough to come away with three hits in the game instead of the three double plays. The Cards slugger also flied out to the warning track in center field and fouled out in the first inning.

But looking at the final tally, Pujols left five runners on base and was responsible for eight outs in the 5–3, 11-inning loss. In his previous 10 season-openers, Pujols had gone 17-of-36, a .472 average, with four homers and 13 RBIs. Two of those homers came in the first game of the 2010 season in Cincinnati.

Maybe it was the law of averages that caught up with Pujols on this day. As far as he was concerned, there was no connection between the results and his contract status.

"I don't think about that," he said of the contract situation. "Flip the page and play the game. It's about playing baseball now, and not what I said a month ago. It's about playing baseball."

The fans, however, could be excused for having a different attitude than Pujols. Some of the comments that were relayed via Twitter during the game were reflective of what people likely would be saying about Pujols all year, magnifying his mistakes and ho-humming his positive accomplishments.

After grounding into the first double play, one fan reportedly tweeted, "That's why he's not worth $30 million." After the game, another fan wrote that because of his combined eight outs, "maybe Pujols' asking price would drop by a million dollars or two."

Had this game happened at any point in the previous 10 years, people would have shrugged their shoulders and said it was just one of those days, knowing there was a greater chance Pujols would come back and hit three homers in the next game than there was of him going 0-for-5 again.

This wasn't just one of those days, however. This was Opening Day, and this was the first game in a season that was unlike any other Pujols had previously experienced. He might not have felt it, but the pressure to perform would be with him throughout 2011 in every game, and during every at-bat, as fans waited to see what would happen at the end of the season. ●

The two best players in franchise history exchange words before the start of the first game of the season. Stan Musial was on hand to see Albert Pujols and the rest of the Cards kick off 2011.

La Russa's Woes

Shingles keep the Cards' skipper out of the dugout

The pain that Albert Pujols felt after going hitless on opening day was not physical, but what Tony La Russa had to deal with soon after was very real. The manager began suffering from what was first diagnosed as chickenpox but was later determined to be a case of shingles, which particularly affected the vision in his right eye.

After trying to deal with the ailment while continuing to manage—and suffering through constant pain—La Russa finally was convinced that he needed to leave the team to seek more intensive medical treatment.

On May 9 he was examined at the Mayo Clinic in Scottsdale, Arizona, where the diagnosis was delivered that he was suffering from shingles. He sat out a six-game road trip to Chicago and Cincinnati, turning the team over to bench coach Joe Pettini.

"It's in his best interest to let the pain subside," said general manager John Mozeliak. "He's going to go on a certain medication to help with the pain. We are hopeful to have him join us on Monday [May 16]. [The doctors] feel the best treatment is rest and time away. We've got to address this, allow the medication to work. [Tony] recognizes it is best for him and the organization."

Pettini was still in communication with La Russa by telephone, and said La Russa would still be making out the lineup and deciding when to give players a day off. He received a voice mail message from La Russa immediately after one of the games in Chicago and joked that he hoped he would not have to take his cell phone with him into the dugout so La Russa could call him during the game.

One lighter moment, which even La Russa appreciated, came when pitcher Kyle Lohse went out to the meeting with the umpires at home plate before one of the games in Chicago dressed in La Russa's number 10 uniform. ●

Tony La Russa jogs out to home plate with the lineup card for the Cardinals' May 16 game against the Phillies. It was La Russa's first time back in the dugout after missing six games while recovering from a case of shingles.

Pujols Goes Down

St. Louis shows resiliency in the face of injuries

Tony La Russa was finally starting to feel better in June when he and everyone else at Busch Stadium watched in horror as Pujols suffered a freak injury during the Cardinals' game on June 19 against Kansas City.

Pujols collided with Royals infielder Wilson Betemit as he attempted to catch a wide throw at first base in the sixth inning of the game. Pujols left hand hit Betemits chest and shoulder, and he fell to the ground in obvious pain.

A CT scan the following day revealed that Pujols had suffered a broken bone in his wrist, and original reports said he would likely be sidelined for about six weeks.

La Russa and several Cardinal players learned about the extent of Pujols injury while they were playing in a charity golf tournament. La Russa was only half joking when he said he was going to go find a quiet place where he could cry.

"It's nothing new to this team this year," Kyle Lohse told the *St. Louis Post-Dispatch*. "We started out spring training taking a big hit, and we've continued to. We've handled it well. Obviously you're not going to get somebody to replace his production. We've just got to piece it together and have guys step in and do the best they can."

The injury came at a time when starting third baseman David Freese already was on the disabled list, having suffered a broken hand when he was hit by a pitch May 1 in a game at Atlanta. Matt Holliday also had missed significant time dealing with a leg injury.

"As a general rule, baseball players are more resilient than others because we deal with failure all the time. That's basically our job—to

Albert Pujols clutches his wrist as he's helped off the field. The injury against the Kansas City Royals cost him more than two weeks but the team continued to play well in his absence.

> ## As a general rule, baseball players are more resilient than others because we deal with failure all the time.
>
> —Lance Berkman

stave off failure," Lance Berkman told the *Post-Dispatch*. "This is a challenge. This is a setback. Heck, we haven't put our full team on the field hardly at all this year. It's hard to name another team out there that could lose its [Nos.] 3 and 4 hitters for a significant amount of time and still be a viable contender. We have. Take [Prince] Fielder and [Ryan] Braun away from Milwaukee. Take [MVP Joey] Votto away from Cincinnati. Do that and I think things would crumble. We have shown such a balanced roster this year that if there is any team equipped to handle it, we are."

As it turned out, Pujols only missed 14 games before he returned to the lineup. The Cardinals were tied for first when he was injured, and led the NL Central by one game when he returned. •

Just weeks after returning from the wrist injury, Pujols collected his 2,000th career hit against the Chicago Cubs on July 29.

Bullpen Mess

Can anyone here actually close out a game?

The Cardinals were able to stay in first place or close to it for the first half of the season despite their abnormal number of injuries, a subpar first half from Pujols, and struggles in the bullpen. Closer Ryan Franklin suffered a blown save on opening day, and that should have been an omen about what was to come in the next few months.

It was not just Franklin who struggled, but as the closer he took the brunt of the criticism from the team's fans. He was moved out of the closer's role and a parade of other relievers tried to fill the job, with mixed results.

For the season, the Cardinals had the misfortune of losing 25 games in their opponents' final at-bat and suffered 13 walk-off losses. They also lost 11 games in which they led in the ninth inning or later.

The 38-year-old Franklin was the one who took the fall for the bullpens failure, getting released by the Cardinals on June 29. He was just 1–4 and had only one save and an 8.46 ERA. He gave up nine homers in only 27⅓ innings in a dramatic fall from grace. Only two years earlier he had made the NL All-Star team and finished the year with a career-high 38 saves.

Before the team got its bullpen woes straightened out later in the year, the team had eight pitchers who saved at least one game and suffered 26 blown saves for the season. Ten pitchers suffered at least one blown save.

Ryan Franklin reacts after giving up a game-tying home run to the San Francisco Giants in April. The bullpen struggled at the start of the year, and Franklin was the man who ended up paying the biggest price when he was released.

Berkman's Surprising Success

Strong first half leads to NL Comeback Player of the Year honor

While the struggling bullpen was a cause for concern, the best story for the Cardinals in the first half of the season was the surprising success of Lance Berkman.

The Cardinals had signed Berkman as a free agent over the winter, even though he had suffered through the worst season of his career in 2010, split between the Astros and the Yankees. The goal was to improve the team's offense, and management was hoping he would be a player who could hit close to .300 with maybe 20-25 homers and around 80 RBIs.

Berkman almost reached those numbers in just the first half of the season.

The 35-year-old outfielder, who went through the most rigorous off-season conditioning program in his career, hit .290 with 24 homers and 63 RBIs in the first half of the season. Berman's performance helped offset one of the worst first halves of a season in Albert Pujols' career, and was good enough for Berkman to be one of the two Cardinals—along with Matt Holliday—selected to start the All-Star game in Phoenix.

Even though Berkman's numbers fell off in the second half of the year, he still was an easy choice as the NL Comeback Player of the Year.

"I wasn't thinking, well, that I had to come back and prove people wrong," said Berkman, who hit just .248 with 14 homers and 58 RBIs as he was coming off knee surgery in

Lance Berkman launches a two-run home run in the eighth inning of a late-August game again the Pittsburgh Pirates.

> **Just the fit seemed perfect for me, just knowing those guys and coming over here, everything I thought it would be. I felt like I fit in pretty quickly."**
>
> **—Lance Berkman**

2010. "That wasn't my attitude at all. I know that that's part of the business and especially when you get to be a little older, that kind of speculation happens all the time."

Nevertheless, it was satisfying for Berkman to have the level of success he enjoyed in his first season with the Cardinals. It was how he hoped the year would go when he made the decision to come to St. Louis.

"I definitely felt like that I would be comfortable here, and the main reason is just the familiarity that I have with the organization from competing against them for a lot of years and knowing these guys," Berkman said. "I'm friends with Adam Wainwright and competed against Carp and Albert, and Matt's a great guy and Skip Schumaker. Just the fit seemed perfect for me, just knowing those guys and coming over here, everything I thought it would be. I felt like I fit in pretty quickly."

Berkman's successful season immediately carried over into the playoffs, as he connected on a home run early in Game 1 of the NLDS.

Trades Reshape Team

Two deals fill pitching and shortstop needs

The Cardinals were tied for first at the All-Star break with a record of six games above .500, at 49–43. They started the second half by continuing to play around .500 for the first 10 days after the break.

That performance was not good enough for general manager John Mozeliak and manager Tony La Russa, who knew the team needed to improve its starting rotation and bullpen if it wanted to continue to contend into September. The Cardinals also wanted to find a better defensive shortstop than Ryan Theriot, hopefully someone who also could fill its need for a leadoff hitter.

In the span of four days before the July 31 trading deadline, Mozeliak made two trades that did all of those things.

The biggest deal came on July 27, when the Cardinals parted ways with starting center fielder and former No. 1 draft pick Colby Rasmus, a player with great potential who for some reason did not seem to be getting better in St. Louis.

It was no secret that Rasmus and La Russa did not get along, and with the emergence of Jon Jay and his ability to play center field, the Cardinals decided it was the right time to move Rasmus, particularly since the deal that sent him to Toronto brought starting pitcher Edwin Jackson (who Toronto had just acquired from the White Sox) and relievers Marc Rzepczynski and Octavio Dotel.

Getting Jackson allowed the Cardinals to move Kyle McClellan out of the starting rotation and into the bullpen, giving La Russa another quality arm to call on late in games.

Some critics of the deal did not believe the Cardinals had received

A strong veteran presence in the rotation, Edwin Jackson provided stability and enjoyed a solid run in the second half of the season.

enough talent in return for Rasmus, who has the raw ability to be a star for years to come. But it was a deal that both Mozeliak and La Russa thought improved the Cardinals at least for the rest of 2011.

"This is a window to win. We feel like we do have some things coming back and draft picks to get in return. Today we feel like we're a better team than we were yesterday," Mozeliak said

All three of the main players who came to St. Louis in the deal did, in fact, turn out to be major contributors to the team over the last two months of the season. At one point later in the year, La Russa said he did not believe the Cardinals would have finished above .500 had they not made the deal.

The second trade pulled off by Mozeliak sent a Double A outfield prospect, Alex Casteallanos, to the Dodgers for veteran shortstop Rafael Furcal. Even though there were questions about Furcal's health and durability, he also proved to be a quality addition to the team, settling in at both the shortstop and leadoff position.

"Every way you look at this, we solidified the places we needed to get stronger, and we did it rather quickly," Mozeliak said.

Both moves were met with positive reviews in the teams clubhouse.

"I think anytime they make moves like they've made it brings excitement to the clubhouse," pitcher Chris Carpenter said. "It shows that they believe we have a shot. Now we just have to go out and play."

Solid defensively and a great option in the leadoff spot, shortstop Rafael Furcal delivered consistency to the middle infield that was lacking early in the season.

Wrong-Way Run

Cards fall 10 games out of playoffs in late August

The immediate impact of the trades was not as positive as John Mozeliak had hoped. Instead of beginning August by closing the two-game gap with the division-leading Brewers, the Cardinals began to go in the opposite direction.

When the Dodgers swept a three-game series against the Cardinals at Busch Stadium, the team woke up on the morning of August 25 to find they were 10 games out of first place in the NL Central and 10 games behind the Atlanta Braves in the wild-card race. The remaining six weeks of the season did not appear to be enough time for the Cardinals to mount a challenge to either the Brewers or Braves.

"When you get beat in a series, especially when you get swept at home, that's as bad as it can get," La Russa said. "We're going to have to reverse that.... The last three, we just got outplayed."

The Cardinals not only were losing, they were worried about a member of their team family. Jeanine Duncan, the wife of pitching coach Dave Duncan, had undergone surgery for a brain tumor a few days earlier,

prompting Duncan to take a leave of absence from the team. No one was certain when he would return.

That was certainly on La Russa's mind when he was asked if the losses had become disheartening. The manager did not like the tone of the question.

"Disheartening is a terrible word to use," La Russa said. "That's a terrible quality. That means you give up, you lose your heart. Disappointed. You get frustrated with some of the ways the games are being played. This league has been forever and ever... as much a sign of your toughness and your character as (it is) your talent. "We're not playing well enough. We're getting beat."

Nobody on the Cardinals or around baseball knew how quickly that was about to change.

Outfielder Skip Schumaker looks frustrated after giving up a home run during an emergency pitching appearance in a blowout loss to the Dodgers in August.

The Climb Back

12 wins in 14 tries put the Cardinals back in the hunt

When the Cardinals opened a three-game series in Milwaukee on August 30, nobody was talking about the possibility that they could catch the Brewers, who now led the division by 10 games.

The Cardinals were not even concerned about the standings at that point. Their only immediate goal was simply to play better, trying to win on that particular day. There was no point, they said, in trying to worry about matters that were outside of their control.

The plan began to pay quick dividends. The Cardinals swept the three games from the Brewers, who had the best home record in the major leagues and had only lost two previous games at home since the All-Star break. A week later they won two of three games against the Brewers in St. Louis and now were only seven games behind the Braves as Atlanta came to town for a three-game series. There were 19 games remaining on St. Louis' schedule.

"It would be nice to make a big dent, and it is significant in that it's the last time we're head to head and you can make some ground up in three days," Berkman said. "But more than that, it's how we play the rest of the year. Even if we make a move to make it interesting, we have to sustain that.

"Everyone in here knows the situation. Everyone knows the math," Berman explained. You understand the desperate straights that we have put ourselves in. And certainly when you're playing a team that you're chasing, you're going to tend to put a little extra weight on those games from an intensity standpoint. But we understand also that we've got to maintain the intensity against the Pirates, against the Cubs, and against whoever we have left on the schedule."

The Cardinals did indeed make it interesting with a three-game sweep of the Braves. Now all of a sudden they were only four games out of the wild-card spot with 16 left to play. Completing their first five-game win-

A pumped-up Albert Pujols is welcomed back to the dugout by Nick Punto and Chris Carpenter after scoring in a late-September game against Houston.

ning streak of the season, Berkman said, had allowed them to enter the realm of possibility.

All of the players knew, however, that the only way they could possibly catch and pass the Braves would be by continuing to win, and hoping that the Braves would continue to lose.

As the Cardinals left on a seven-game trip to Pittsburgh and Philadelphia, nobody knew what the standings would look like when the team returned home a week later.

"I can't pinpoint why it's happening now. But what's happening is we're beating some pretty good teams," said second baseman Skip Schumaker. "I don't know why it took this long. But better now than never."

Jason Motte, who saved the final game against Atlanta, was one of the reasons for the team's success. After earning his first save of the year on August 28, Motte was being used more and more by La Russa to close out games, even though the manager refused to officially name Motte the closer.

That didn't matter to Motte, as long as the Cardinals continued to win.

"We looked at it like we weren't out of it," Motte said. "And we're still not out of it until the last game of the season or until we're eliminated and can't come back…. We have to play, just worry about ourselves and try to win games."

That was exactly what they did. After winning five of the seven games on the road trip, the Cardinals came home and won two in a row over the Mets. The win on September 21 came courtesy of a three-run homer by the hometown kid, David Freese. It was the Cardinals 12th win out of 14 games, and combined with the Braves eighth loss in 12 games, cut their wild-card deficit to one game with seven left to play.

"That's why you keep grinding it out, for things like that to happen," Freese said. "Playoff baseball in St. Louis is expected out of you and I wouldn't want it any other way. I always said if I don't get to the playoffs as a Cardinal that might be my only regret."

Whether the Cardinals would be playing playoff games or not in 2011 would be determined by what happened in the final week of the season. ●

Edwin Jackson congratulates Jaime Garcia after a strong outing from Garcia ended in the eighth inning against the Mets on September 21.

The Final Stretch

Pujols and the Cards stay focused on a postseason berth

The Cardinals knew there was little margin for error if they had any chance of catching the Braves. One loss could mean the difference between going to the playoffs or staying home.

Which is why losing a game in the manner they did against the Mets on September 22 could have been devastating. Leading 6–2 going to the ninth inning, the Cardinals saw the Mets score six times in the final inning to win the game 8–6.

The Cardinals were two outs away from a win which would have cut Atlanta's lead to one game when Furcal committed a critical error and Motte could not find the strike zone, walking three batters, to fuel the Mets rally.

"We're disappointed. We're upset," La Russa said. "But you make a big mistake if you think we're heartbroken. We didn't mail in the series win. We played our (tails) off and couldn't close it down. It's disappointing. Don't make a mistake and say we're heartbroken. Our heart is beating."

A loss the following night to the Cubs also was frustrating, but then the Cardinals came out on the other end of a game that it appeared they were going to lose. Trailing 1–0 going to the bottom of the ninth, a single, a stolen base, a throwing error, and three walks by Carlos Marmol allowed the Cardinals to tie the game. Marmol then uncorked a wild pitch, allowing the winning run to score from third.

"Dramatic. Important," La Russa said. "If we would have lost that one, we were eight-ball time. We're in it. That's part of the excitement. We're in it."

Even without the playoff possibility looming over them, the Cardinals knew their game on Sunday, September 25 could turn out to be a memorable day. It was the final home game of the year, before a season-ending three-game trip to Houston. It also could have been Albert Pujols' final game as a Cardinal at Busch Stadium.

Aware of the situation, the 40,000-plus fans in attendance rose to

The bullpen played a key role in the Cardinals' comeback, erasing fears that may have arisen after their slow start to the season.

give Pujols a prolonged standing ovation when the came to bat in the first
inning. Chicago pitcher Randy Wells,
from nearby Belleville, Illinnois,
stepped off the mound to give Pujols
time to acknowledge the cheers.

Pujols expected some recogni-
tion from the fans, but he became a
little emotional about the warmth of
the greeting.

"I've been in the situation before
where you have the fans standing up
and cheering you," Pujols said. "It
was a little more special, but you still
try to make sure you stay focused. At
the end it's not about me, it's about
our ballclub and we are doing something pretty special this month and
hopefully we can continue to do that
the next three days and see where we
are on Wednesday."

Pujols finished the day 0-for-4,
the first time he failed to reach base
in 41 games. His average for the year
was an even .300, and he was two
RBIs shy of reaching 100 for the 11th
consecutive year.

"Our season's not over," Pujols
said. "I just want to make sure that
I stay focused and do what I need to
do. I know I didn't contribute the way
I wanted to help our ballclub, but the
win was huge for us."

There was no denying Pujols'
statements that he was focused en-
tirely on the Cardinals attempt to
chase down the Braves for the wild-
card spot in the playoffs and not on
where he will be playing next season.

"I m still wearing a Cardinal uniform," he said. "Until they take this
jersey away from me I'm going to
continue to try to do the best I can for
the city and the organization."

It was a true team effort in September.
Chris Carpenter is seen here helping
his own cause with a two-run single on
September 13 against the Pirates.

The Final Night

Win over Houston leads to "happy flight" to playoffs

A split of the two first two games in Houston, combined with the Braves losing four game in a row left the two teams tied for the wild-card spot as the season reached game number 162 on the final day of the year.

The Cardinals knew they now controlled their own destiny A win would guarantee them no worse than a one-game playoff against the Braves, with the game to be played in St. Louis, no matter what Atlanta did in its final game of the season at home against the Phillies.

With the wild-card spot in the American League also to be determined by games between Boston and Baltimore and the Yankees at Tampa Bay, the stage was set for potentially one of the most dramatic days in MLB history.

And as it turned out, the Cardinals game would produce the least amount of tension of the night.

A five-run first inning staked Carpenter to an early lead, and he steamrolled the Astros for an 8–0 win. The game ended so quickly that the Cardinals had to sit in the visiting clubhouse at Minute Maid Park, waiting for the Braves game to end before they knew their fate.

The Braves game went to the 13th inning. Finally, the Phillies took the lead on an RBI single by Hunter Pence, and when Freddie Freeman grounded into a double play to end the game, the Cardinals celebration was on.

The finish of the game in Atlanta was combined with dramatic endings just minutes later in Baltimore and Tampa Bay, which knocked the Red Sox out of the playoffs and gave Tampa Bay the AL wild-card victory.

"We weren't supposed to be here," said Schumaker. "I still don't know how we did it, but we did it."

They did it by refusing to lose when they couldn't lose, by winning 23 of their final 39 games and by hav-

Chris Carpenter celebrates with Yadier Molina after his impressive two-hit shutout performance against the Astros that secured the National League's wild card on the last day of the season.

ing the Braves experience the misfortune of one of the greatest collapses in MLB history.

"We had nothing to lose. We were already out of it," Carpenter said about the final month comeback. "People were telling us we were done. We decided to go out and play and not embarrass ourselves and do what we can. We played ourselves back into it. The way these guys have played the past month and a half has been amazing, every single night grinding, playing their butts off, not giving up. We continued to give ourselves an opportunity and now we are here."

Perhaps the only disappointment of the night was that Pujols, trying to hit .300 and drive in 100 runs for the 11th consecutive year to go along with his 30-plus homers, finished just short of both goals. He had one RBI in the game, but that left him with a .299 average and 99 RBIs.

That was not on Pujols mind as he celebrated with his teammates, however.

"It's unbelievable," Pujols said. "Twenty eight days ago we were eight games out. Everybody thought out season was over. But it isn't over until you play 162 games."

The victory was the Cardinals' 90th of the season, a total many thought they would never reach back on the dark February day when Adam Wainwright was injured.

Pitching coach Dave Duncan was back with the team for the final game, another reason why everybody on the Cardinals was smiling.

After the Cardinals lost a game in Milwaukee on August 3, Furcal came up with the idea that the team needed to win its final game every time they were about to get on an airplane to go home or to their next city. He termed those trips "happy flights" and it became one of the team's rallying cries in September, along with their good luck charm, a pet tortoise owned by Allen Craig and nicknamed Torty.

Starting on August 7 after a win in Miami, the Cardinals won 11 consecutive games when they were getting ready to board a plane. The flight taking them home from Houston on this night would be happy indeed.

This happy flight was taking the Cardinals to the playoffs, a trip they never thought they would be making just six weeks earlier.

"We felt like we played more relaxed this month than in any other month," Schumaker said. "We're having fun. We're trying to do our best and see what happens. We haven't pressed. And I don't think we're going to press in the playoffs. A lot of us have been here before. We're going to give it our best shot and see what happens. We've got an extremely tough task ahead of us, but I like our chances."

Allen Craig celebrates after his home run late against the Astros. It provided an insurance run after a five-run first inning all but buried Houston.

Matt Holliday

Outfielder overcomes odd maladies to post solid season

In 2011, Matt Holliday thought he had experienced everything that could possibly have happened to him over the course of a single season.

He underwent an emergency appendectomy following Opening Day. Later in the year he hurt a leg muscle, and then he suffered another injury when he was preparing to lift a weight, not actually while lifting it.

Then came the game against the Dodgers on August 22 at Busch Stadium, when Holliday was standing in left field and started experiencing a very uncomfortable feeling in his right ear.

A moth had flown into his ear and become stuck. Holliday had to come out of the game, and the clubs medical personnel finally were able to pull the moth out of Holliday's ear with a pair of tweezers.

"I'm not sure it could get any weirder," Holliday said about all of the medical woes that afflicted him during the season.

"I knew it was a moth, by the sound of the flutter," Holliday said. "I was just standing there and all of a sudden there's a moth fluttering in my ear like crazy. I started shaking my head, like you do when you have water in your ear but I said, 'That's not working.' I don't think my glove was on for one pitch because I was trying to get it out. But it was like, 'I can't handle this.' That's when I called time out."

Holliday was back in the lineup the following day but he was not finished with strange injuries.

A couple of weeks later, on September 13, Holliday suffered an inflamed tendon on the middle finger of his right hand while swinging a bat in the on-deck circle.

It was first thought the injury might be severe enough to sideline Holliday for the rest of the season, but he was able to return and play in four of the final regular-season games, although he pulled himself from the lineup on September 27 because of the pain in his hand, and his concern that he might not be able to make a throw in a crucial situation.

"It's strange because I can do certain things and have little or no discomfort, and there are other things that really cause it to grab," Holliday said. "There's not a whole lot I can do about it right now."

Playing through his various injuries and ailments, Holliday finished the year with a .296 average, the first time he did not hit .300 in his three years as a Cardinal. He hit 22 homers, his lowest total since 2005, and drove in only 75 runs, his fewest since his 2004 rookie season with Colorado. Holliday's 124 games also were the fewest he had played since his rookie year. ●

Matt Holliday has been a major boost to the Cardinals' lineup since being acquired from Oakland in 2009. When the team first acquired him, they went on a 20–6 run through August en route to the Central Division title.

The Final Night

Win over Houston leads to "happy flight" to playoffs

A split of the two first two games in Houston, combined with the Braves losing four game in a row left the two teams tied for the wild-card spot as the season reached game number 162 on the final day of the year.

The Cardinals knew they now controlled their own destiny A win would guarantee them no worse than a one-game playoff against the Braves, with the game to be played in St. Louis, no matter what Atlanta did in its final game of the season at home against the Phillies.

With the wild-card spot in the American League also to be determined by games between Boston and Baltimore and the Yankees at Tampa Bay, the stage was set for potentially one of the most dramatic days in MLB history.

And as it turned out, the Cardinals game would produce the least amount of tension of the night.

A five-run first inning staked Carpenter to an early lead, and he steamrolled the Astros for an 8–0 win. The game ended so quickly that the Cardinals had to sit in the visiting clubhouse at Minute Maid Park, waiting for the Braves game to end before they knew their fate.

The Braves game went to the 13th inning. Finally, the Phillies took the lead on an RBI single by Hunter Pence, and when Freddie Freeman grounded into a double play to end the game, the Cardinals celebration was on.

The finish of the game in Atlanta was combined with dramatic endings just minutes later in Baltimore and Tampa Bay, which knocked the Red Sox out of the playoffs and gave Tampa Bay the AL wild-card victory.

"We weren't supposed to be here," said Schumaker. "I still don't know how we did it, but we did it."

They did it by refusing to lose when they couldn't lose, by winning 23 of their final 39 games and by having the Braves experience the misfortune of one of the greatest collapses in MLB history.

"We had nothing to lose. We were already out of it," Carpenter said about the final month comeback. "People were telling us we were done. We decided to go out and play and not embarrass ourselves and do what we can. We played ourselves back into it. The way these guys have played the past month and a half has been amazing, every single night grinding, playing their butts off, not giving up. We continued to give ourselves an opportunity and now we are here."

Perhaps the only disappointment of the night was that Pujols, trying to hit .300 and drive in 100 runs for the 11th consecutive year to go along with his 30-plus homers, finished just short of both goals. He had one RBI in the game, but that left him with a .299 average and 99 RBIs.

That was not on Pujols mind as he celebrated with his teammates, however.

A jubilant Chris Carpenter celebrates his complete-game shutout over the Astros. The 8–0 victory in the season finale kept the Cards in the playoff hunt.

"It's unbelievable," Pujols said. "Twenty eight days ago we were eight games out. Everybody thought out season was over. But it isn't over until you play 162 games."

The victory was the Cardinals' 90th of the season, a total many thought they would never reach back on the dark February day when Adam Wainwright was injured.

Pitching coach Dave Duncan was back with the team for the final game, another reason why everybody on the Cardinals was smiling.

After the Cardinals lost a game in Milwaukee on August 3, Furcal came up with the idea that the team needed to win its final game every time they were about to get on an airplane to go home or to their next city. He termed those trips "happy flights" and it became one of the team's rallying cries in September, along with their good luck charm, a pet tortoise owned by Allen Craig and nicknamed Torty.

Starting on August 7 after a win in Miami, the Cardinals won 11 consecutive games when they were getting ready to board a plane. The flight taking them home from Houston on this night would be happy indeed.

This happy flight was taking the Cardinals to the playoffs, a trip they never thought they would be making just six weeks earlier.

"We felt like we played more relaxed this month than in any other month," Schumaker said. "We're having fun. We're trying to do our best and see what happens. We haven't pressed. And I don't think we're going to press in the playoffs. A lot of us have been here before. We're going to give it our best shot and see what happens. We've got an extremely tough task ahead of us, but I like our chances."

Albert Pujols (left) congratulates Allen Craig after Craig's ninth-inning solo homer wrapped up the scoring in the Cardinals' 8-0 win over Houston.

NATIONAL LEAGUE
Playoffs Recap

The Cardinals looked dead in the water in August but a late surge in the regular-season pushed them into the playoffs. Once there, they upset the Phillies, earning a meeting with the Brewers in the National League Championship Series.

National League Division Series
Game 1: Phillies 11, Cardinals 6

The Cardinals' "reward" for winning the wild-card spot in the playoffs was a first-round match-up against the Philadelphia Phillies, a team that had the best record in baseball during the regular season, winning a franchise-record 102 games.

It was not a surprise to manager Tony La Russa or any of his players that nobody expected the Cardinals to win the series. Many observers did not even pick them to win a game in the best-of-five series.

That pessimism was not shared in the visiting clubhouse, where La Russa often is at his best when he can position his team as "us against the world," and that was the rallying cry he intended to use in this series.

The series seemed to get off to a good start for the underdog Cardinals when Lance Berkman hit a three-run homer off Phillies' ace Roy Halladay in the first inning of the opener. Their joy was short-lived, however, as Halladay settled down, the Phillies bats

came to life, and the NL East champs posted an 11–6 victory.

St. Louis starting pitcher Kyle Lohse and the rest of the Cardinals learned there would be very little margin for error in the series. Lohse made only two bad pitches, both hanging change-ups in the sixth inning. St, Louis native Ryan Howard hit the first one for a three-run homer that put the Phillies on top 4–3. Two batters later, Raul Ibanez hit the second one for a two-run homer to increase the lead to 6–3 en route to the opening victory.

"It boils down to two bad pitches," Lohse said. "The inning started off with a couple balls that just found the hole and after that, it ended with a couple of really bad pitches. Pretty simple.

"I feel like I could let them know a change-up is coming if I execute it it's going to result in a good thing but I threw them right down the middle. I just hung them. My change-up, I'll take my chances in any count with any batter. It just didn't work out today."

The playoff opener didn't quite go according to plan for the Cardinals. Here, Lance Berkman reacts after striking out in the sixth inning.

National League Division Series

Game 2: Cardinals 5, Phillies 4

The Game 1 loss meant that the Cardinals had to win the second game if they wanted to accomplish their goal of splitting the series' first two games in Philadelphia. The team felt good about sending its best starter, Chris Carpenter, to the mound even though he was pitching on three days rest for the first time in his career.

The move did not work out well, however, as Carpenter struggled with his control and quickly fell behind 4–0. He ended up logging just three innings before giving way to Fernando Salas. Making the chances of a comeback even tougher was the fact that Cliff Lee, who had enjoyed a spectacular regular season, was pitching for the Phillies.

In the first sign of what would turn out to be a trend in the postseason, the St. Louis bullpen shut down the Phillies, retiring 17 of the final 19 batters. The Cardinals began to chip away, tying the game on an RBI single by Jon Jay in the sixth inning. A triple by Allan Craig and single by Pujols in the seventh secured the 5–4 victory.

"We've been doing this all year. We don't give up," said reliever Jason Motte after closing out the game in the ninth. "People counted us out, (but) we kind of went out there and just kept playing hard."

The Cardinals knew how tough it would be to win this game after they spotted Lee the early lead, but they knew they were still going to go to the plate and try to get hits. They ended up knocking Lee around to the tune of five runs on 12 hits.

"That doesn't happen very often but neither does coming from 8½ back with a month to play," said outfielder Lance Berkman.

Albert Pujols comes up with a ball off the bat of Shane Victorino early in Game 2.

The fans arrived early at Busch Stadium before Game 3, packing the stadium to support their Cardinals.

National League Division Series
Game 3: Phillies 3, Cardinals 2

The series moved to St. Louis for Game 3, and it quickly turned into a battle of managerial wits. Watching Charlie Manuel of the Phillies and Tony La Russa of the Cardinals send in pinch-hitters, make pitching changes, and order intentional walks offered a fascinating study in baseball strategy.

"It was two really good managers managing a very tough game," said the Cardinals' Skip Schumaker. "You've got to appreciate it. That's why postseason baseball is so much fun."

This night turned out to be more fun for the Phillies than the Cardinals after they escaped with a pulsating 3–2 victory, which put them ahead 2–1 in the best-of-five series.

Starting with La Russa's decision to intentionally walk Hunter Pence with two outs and a runner on second in the sixth—to bring Cardinal-killer Ryan Howard to the plate—the two managers went back and fourth for the final four innings of the game. They made a combined 15 decisions over the game's final 22 outs, moves that largely determined the outcome of the context.

The decision to walk Pence proved to be a good one, as Howard grounded weakly to first, but the battle of managerial wits was just beginning.

The biggest decision of the game turned out to be Manuel sending Ben Francisco up to bat for Hamels with two outs and runners on first and second in the seventh inning of the scoreless game. La Russa had just ordered an intentional walk to Carlos Ruiz, even though he knew Manuel would bring in a pinch-hitter for Hamels, who had thrown 117 pitches.

Instead of countering that move with a right-hander out of the bullpen, La Russa elected to leave Garcia in the game, knowing Francisco was only 1-for-9 lifetime off the left-handed pitcher. Francisco made Manuel look like the genius, hitting a 1–0 pitch into the left field bleachers for a three-run homer.

Skip Schumaker reacts after his catch in the ninth inning was originally ruled a hit. After the umpires conferred, it was confirmed that Schumaker had, indeed, come up with the stellar grab.

According to BaseballReference. com, Francisco's homer was only the seventh time in MLB postseason history a pinch-hitter hit a three-run homer or grand slam in the seventh inning of a game or later. The last time it happened was by J.T. Snow of the Giants in the 2000 NLCS against the Mets.

In Francisco's major-league career, he had hit only one previous pinch-hit home run, in 2007 when he played for the Indians. It also was only the third overall pinch-hit of his career and, according to the Elias Sports Bureau, Francisco became the first player in postseason history to hit a pinch-hit home run that snapped a scoreless tie.

"You have to have guts to play this game and to manage," Schumaker said. "Tony doesn't lack guts."

What ultimately spoiled La Russa's 67th birthday were the 14 runners the Cardinals left on base and their combined 3-for-12 performance with runners in scoring position.

"You can only pull a rabbit out of a hat a couple of times," Berkman said. "We gave ourselves a chance and we just didn't do it. Somebody was going to be up 2–1 after today. We wish it had been us, but that's the way it is. The season didn't end today. We're going to come back out tomorrow and see what happens."

Jaime Garcia grounded out—and broke his bat—while supporting his pitching effort with a little offense in the fourth inning of Game 3.

National League Division Series
Game 4: Cardinals 5, Phillies 3

One of the Cardinals who had been frustrated by his performance in the first three games of the series was third baseman David Freese, who had only two hits in 12 at-bats and had struck out six times. As Freese drove to Busch Stadium for Game 4, with the Cardinals facing elimination with another loss, he didn't know La Russa was meeting to discuss the lineup for the game, including the possibility of playing Daniel Descalso at third in place of Freese.

The vote among the coaches was to keep Freese in the lineup, and that turned out to be a great decision for the Cardinals.

Freese doubled in the fourth inning to drive in two runs and put his team ahead, 3–2. He then made certain the pitching staff had more than enough runs to work with by adding a two-run homer in the sixth, powering the Cardinals to a 5–3 win.

After striking out again in the second, Freese went down to the video room and looked at some of his at-bats. Not typically a player who spends much time watching himself on tape, Freese noticed that he was not keeping his front foot on the ground as he began his approach to the ball, a key for him to get the timing he needs to hit.

Making a conscious effort to keep the foot on the ground in his next at-bat, which came with runners on first and second and one out in the fourth, Freese lined Roy Oswalt's first pitch into the left field corner, driving in both runs.

Two innings later, Freese got to live out a dream he had many times growing up in West County, Freese connected on a 1-0 pitch, sending it 424 feet into the right centerfield seats. Even though Freese was born in Texas, his family moved to the area

David Freese celebrates with Matt Holliday after Freese's two-run homer in the sixth inning of Game 4.

"This is what you worked for, and just to do this in front of the fans of St. Louis and a bunch of family and friends is amazing," —David Freese

when he was three years old, making him the first St. Louisian to hit a post-season home run for the Cardinals since Mike Shannon did so in Game 7 of the 1968 World Series.

A family from Ohio even made sure that Freese had the souvenir from the best moment of his baseball career, returning the ball to him after the game in exchange for a photo.

"This is what you worked for, and just to do this in front of the fans of St. Louis and a bunch of family and friends is amazing," Freese said.

As happy as Freese was, his team-mates were just as happy for him.

"Nobody works harder or has been through more than David," said Skip Schumaker. "I said in spring training that a healthy David Freese would be the MVP of our team be-cause he helps out the lineup so much and gives it so much depth. The guy is a stud, he really is. No one is happier for him than me." •

Already in a frenzy, the fans at Busch Stadium react loudly after the home run by David Freese. It was a breakout performance for the third baseman, as he drove in all but one of the Cardinals' runs in the 5–4 victory.

National League Division Series
Game 5: Cardinals 1, Phillies 0

The Cardinals' win in Game 4 set up a contest baseball fans everywhere had been waiting for—the first time former Toronto teammates and good friends Chris Carpenter and Roy Halladay had ever gone to the mound to face each other. And they were doing it knowing the loser was going home for the winter.

The two pitchers first met in 1996, in spring training, each a former first-round draft pick of the Blue Jays. They bonded very quickly and two years later they both were in the majors.

"We fished a bunch," Carpenter said of some of the duo's early activities together. "We spent spring training one year, me and him and my wife and his wife before we had kids, renting in the same condo. We owned a boat together that spring training, and we'd fish every night and sometimes get up and go fishing in the morning

before anything had to start. Golf, I mean, we did all kinds of different things together."

They also of course bonded on the baseball field, cheering for each other and learning at the same time how to succeed as pitchers.

"I really felt like we grew together," Halladay said. "Coming up we both kind of struggled with—we were supposed to come in and lead this team and be these great pitchers right out of the gate, and I think it was tough for both of us not really knowing how to go about that. I really did feel like we kind of learned together, more mentally how to approach the game and how to play the game, and it was a lot of fun."

In Halladay, Carpenter found a person he could talk to and identify with and—just as important—learn from, not just about baseball, but about life as well.

"It was not about stuff, it was about being able to control our minds,"

A locked-in Chris Carpenter throws a pitch during the first inning of the epic pitching duel in Game 5 of the National League Division Series.

Carpenter said last week about those late-night conversations. "When I was a young kid, it was all about 'oh, man, I've got Joe Schmo behind the plate that doesn't call a strike and doesn't like young guys' or whatever it was, 'wind is blowing out here in Baltimore, what am I going to do, these guys are going to crush me, I've got no chance,' it was all about confidence and having to eliminate distractions. We went through a lot those times together and learned together, so those are similarities between us."

According to research by the Elias Sports Bureau, the game was only the third time since the Cy Young Award was first handed out in 1956 that two former winners had opposed each other in the deciding game of a postseason series. Both of the other match-ups came in the American League, both involving Pedro Martinez. He was paired against Barry Zito in the fifth game of a Division Series in 2003, and in 2007 Martinez went up against Roger Clemens in the seventh game of the AL Championship Series.

Usually when a game receives as much buildup and hype as was the case with the 2011 NLDS Game 5, the actual event turns out to be a letdown. That certainly was not the case on this night, however.

In what will be remembered as a classic and one of the best-pitched games in the history of postseason baseball, Carpenter outdueled Halladay and pitched the Cardinals into

The celebration was on for the Cardinals as they finished off the Phillies with a 1-0 win in Philadelphia.

the NL Championship Series against the Milwaukee Brewers. Carpenter hurled a three-hit shutout and the Cardinals' first two batters, Rafael Furcal and Skip Schumaker, produced the only run in the game.

It was only the third 1–0 victory in an elimination game in the history of Major League Baseball, joining the Yankees' victory over the Giants in Game 7 of the 1962 World Series and Game 7 of the 1991 World Series, when Jack Morris of the Twins pitched 10 shutout innings in beating John Smoltz and the Braves.

"It was an unbelievable night," said Carpenter, who did not walk a batter and retired 10 of the final 11 batters he faced (the only runner reaching on an error by Yadier Molina after a dropped third strike) in eliminating the favored Phillies. Carpenter retired the first batter in eight of his nine innings of work and only once allowed two runners in an inning—in the fourth—but got out of the jam when Raul Ibanez flied out to the warning track in right.

Watching the game on television at a restaurant in Scottsdale, Arizona, was Tim Wilken, the scouting director for the Cubs. Previously, he had held the same job with the Blue Jays, and was responsible for drafting both Carpenter and Halladay.

"That was a pretty darn good game," said Wilken, "probably better than you could have expected. Needless to say it was a wonderful evening. It was two warriors and two wonderful human beings. Unbelievable."

Wilken said he was a little worried about Carpenter before the game, wondering if his subpar performance in Game 2 was a sign that the wear and tear of the regular season was getting to the 36-year-old pitcher. Carpenter, in fact, pitched the most innings in the National League this season.

"In the back of my mind I was hoping it would be a good game," Wilken said.

It turned out that Wilken did not need to worry. How good was this game? Here are just a few reasons why it will long be remembered:

- Carpenter became the third pitcher in postseason history to throw a shutout, allowing three hits or less, in a clinching game. The other two were Johnny Kucks of the Yankees in Game 7 of the 1956 World Series and Sandy Koufax of the Dodgers in Game 7 of the 1965 World Series.
- It was only the third complete game shutout ever pitched by a Cardinals pitcher in a clinching game in the postseason, joining games by Dizzy Dean in the 1934 World Series and Danny Cox in the 1987 NLCS.
- It was the 42nd 1–0 game in MLB postseason history, but was only the second time the Cardinals won a game 1–0 in their 190 postseason games. That was game six of the 1987 NLCS versus the Giants, when John Tudor, Todd Worrell, and Ken Dayley combined on the shutout.
- Carpenter had made 339 starts in his career before this game, including the regular season and postseason, and he had never won a 1–0 complete game.
- It was the first time the Phillies had lost a 1–0 game in their home stadium in three years.

It was a pretty special night indeed. Said Cardinals manager Tony La Russa, "I think he [Carpenter] will remember that forever, and so will the Cardinals' fans."

Wilken knew that Carpenter, Halladay, and former Cardinals pitcher Pat Hentgen, also a former teammate and close friend, already had planned a fishing trip together a few weeks after the conclusion of the season. He knows this game certainly will come up, and probably the first thing Carpenter will want to talk about was his eighth-inning single off Halladay.

"I am sure that will come up," Wilken said. "If Chris doesn't bring it up I'm sure Pat will.

"It was a wonderful evening as far as being a viewer. I'm just glad I had the opportunity to know both of these gentlemen, and I say that with great respect. They are both wonderful human beings. I haven't seen Chris for a while, and hopefully will run into him somewhere. I can't say enough about both of them. Hopefully Chris will carry that torch all the way through the World Series."

The true agony of defeat. In a much-replayed clip, Ryan Howard suffered not only from a series-ending ground out but also a torn Achilles tendon after stumbling while running to first base.

National League Championship Series

Game 1: Brewers 9, Cardinals 6

Cardinals' starter Jamie Garcia was cruising along with a 5–2 lead going into the fifth inning of the NLCS Game 1, when the contest changed so fast neither La Russa or anybody else had time to react.

In the span of three pitchers, the Brewers went from trailing by three runs to leading by a run. After Corey Hart singled to lead off the inning, Jerry Hairston worked the count to 2–2 before he doubled.

That double ignited the attack, and on the next two pitches that Garcia threw, Ryan Braun hit a ground-rule double and Prince Fielder followed with a long home run. Even after La Russa was able to change pitchers, Yuniesky Betancourt hit a two-run homer off Dotel and the Brewers put away the Game 1 victory.

The Brewers ended up with five extra-base hits in the fifth inning, tying a postseason record.

"It was just bam, bam, bam," La Russa said. "He made three straight pitches in the middle of the plate, and they didn't miss any of them. It was a weird inning."

The Cardinals' last chance to mount a comeback died in the seventh inning, when Pujols grounded into a double play.

David Freese fires a rocket to first base to nab Ryan Braun in the third inning of the first game of the NLCS.

David Freese

Hometown hero credits one-year break from baseball for his success

David Freese walked away from baseball when he was 18 years old. After graduating from Lafayette High School in the St. Louis suburbs, he decided he needed a break and wanted to attend the University of Missouri as a regular freshman, without the pressures created by the sport he had played all of his life.

One of his coaches sent another Lafayette graduate, Ryan Howard—three years older than Freese—to try to talk Freese out of that decision. The two talked for about 30 minutes, but Freese had his mind made up.

"I guess I didn't listen to him too much," Freese said of that meeting. "He was just trying to be like a big brother, to make sure I was making the right decision. He said God had a plan and wished me luck in whatever I did."

It took a year away from the game before Freese realized how much he missed playing baseball. He transferred from Missouri to Meramec Community College, then went to South Alabama and was drafted by the San Diego Padres.

A trade to the Cardinals in 2007 accelerated his path to the major leagues, but his success was interrupted by a car accident, surgery on both ankles, and finally a broken hand suffered when he was hit by a pitch.

All of these challenges made him appreciate what happened in the 2011 postseason, when he followed up his key home run in the National League Division Series by having an even better series against the Milwaukee Brewers.

Freese hit .545 in the six-game National League Championship Series, extending his postseason hitting streak to 10 games—one game longer than his longest streak in the regular season. He hit three homers and drove in nine runs as he was named series MVP. The only other player in MLB postseason history who has put up those kinds of numbers for a single series was Lou Gehrig of the Yankees in the 1928 World Series.

Adding in the Division Series, Freese posted a .425 average with four homers and an NL-high 14 RBIs in 11 games.

Freese doesn't know where he would be now if he had not walked away from baseball a decade ago, but he knows where he would have not been.

"I can tell you right now if I had kept playing I would not be here right now," Freese said.

Having that success for his hometown team, the team he cheered for as a youngster—including when he attended a game in the 1996 NLCS against the Braves when he was 13 years old—just made the moment all the more special.

"Not too many people get a chance to do this in their hometown," Freese said. "It's an unbelievable feeling. To be a part of this team, this group of guys, this organization, means a lot. It's a dream come true." ●

Freese shows off his sweet swing on what might have been his best night of the season. This two-run homer was a game changer on his four-RBI night in Game 4 of the Division Series against the Phillies.

National League Championship Series

Game 2: Cardinals 12, Brewers 3

It was almost as if Albert Pujols wanted to take his disappointment over that rally-killing double play in Game 1 out on the Brewers, because that was exactly what he did in Game 2.

Pujols began his day with a two-run homer in the first inning, the first postseason home run he had hit since Game 1 of the 2006 World Series, a span of 13 games and 47 at-bats. He got two more RBIs with a double in his next at-bat in the fourth, then another double produced Pujols' fifth RBI of the night. He added one more double, before finally getting a cheer out of the Miller Park crowd when he grounded out in the eighth.

His three doubles, home run, and five RBIs helped him become only the fourth player in MLB history to record four extra-base hits in a postseason game and the first to do it since Hideki Matsui in the 2004 AL Championship Series.

"You learn from the mistakes that you make," Pujols said. "[Game 1] was so tough, going to bed I was just thinking some of the opportunity that I could help our ballclub to win."

La Russa was not surprised at Pujols' night, noting before the game that he could turn out to be the offensive star.

"He takes it personally," La Russa said. "He was fine-tuning his stroke. He wasn't really trying to hit the ball out of the park, He was just thinking about how he could have better at-bats. He's such a pro, so smart."

The win pulled the Cardinals even in the series as they headed home to St. Louis for Game 3.

Albert Pujols reacts emphatically after doubling in Game 2.

National League Championship Series
Game 3: Cardinals 4, Brewers 3

Sometime between the second and fourth inning of Game 3 of the NLCS at Busch Stadium in St. Louis, Milwaukee manager Ron Roenicke got the seven-word memo. Printed in very big, bold letters, the message was simple and direct: "Do not let Albert Pujols beat us."

But by then, it was too late.

Thanks to a four-run first inning, which included an RBI double by Pujols, and 12 consecutive outs by the bullpen, the Cardinals won game three 4–3 to take a two-games-to-one lead in the best-of-seven series.

Pujols' first-inning double, on the first pitch he saw from Yovani Gallardo, came with first base open—and with Roenicke knowing that Pujols has tattooed Gallardo over his career: 12 hits in 27 at-bats, including 10 hits in the last 18 times the two had faced each other.

Gallardo seemed to come a little unglued after Pujols' two-run double, walking Matt Holliday and Lance Berkman, and two more runs scored before Gallardo finally got out of the inning. That would turn out to be all of the scoring the Cardinals would need on this night.

The four runs in the first marked the fifth consecutive playoff game in which the Cardinals scored in the first inning, the first team to have such a streak since the 2004 Red Sox. In the first three games of the NLCS, the Cardinals scored seven runs in the opening inning against the Brewers. In the first inning of those three games, Pujols went 3-for-3 with three RBIs and two runs scored.

"He hit a great pitch," Roenicke said. "It was a nice curveball down in the zone, and he drove it to left center."

It was Pujols' seventh double of this postseason, tying the record for most doubles in a postseason. His second-inning single did no further

The Brewers' Casey McGehee is unable to lay off the pitch and Yadier Molina begins to celebrate as the Cardinals take Game 3 of the NLCS.

damage, but may have prompted a shift in the Brewers' pitching strategy going forward in the series: Pujols was intentionally walked in both of his other two at-bats in the game, in the fourth and sixth innings, and each time Matt Holliday followed with an inning-ending strikeout.

Holliday swung at six pitches which were out of the strike zone during the two at-bats, stranding four runners on base as the Cardinals failed to add to their one-run lead.

"I think when it really makes sense, we'll do it," Roenicke said of walking Pujols intentionally. "I don't want to just put him on to put him on. You saw we put him on with a guy on third base and the next thing you know it's second and third instead of first and third. They get a base hit there, they are scoring two runs instead of one.

"We are going to pick our spots where we think we need to do it. If it comes up, when it makes sense, then we'll try to put him on. He's scary when he's hitting everything and we make good pitches and he's still hitting them. He's done a lot of damage against us."

Which is why, even though Roenicke hates the intentional walk, it makes perfect sense for him to hold up the four fingers almost any time Pujols comes to the plate.

The strategy to pitch around Pujols—who was hitting .636 (7-for-11) at that point in the NLCS—did not come without risk.

"I think we have a bunch of premier hitters, stacked one after the other, and generally somebody's going to do something," said Lance Berkman. "If you don't have seven or eight quality hitters, then they can focus and say 'this guy's not going to beat us' and then you're stuck. The thing that makes our team dangerous is that you can walk Albert all you want, but then you have Matt, myself, Molina, Freese. It's tough. It puts teams in a bad spot when everything's clicking.

"I don't think anybody thinks as highly of Albert as I do. I think he is probably the greatest hitter ever, doing it in this ballpark and in this era. It's a worldwide game, we have players from all over but that having been said, I'm having a difficult time walking anybody to pitch to Matt Holliday. He's won a batting title, he's been an NLCS MVP. You might get him a couple of times, but if you keep doing it he's going to get you." ●

The ball leaps off the bat of John Jay as he connects on his first-inning, run-scoring double.

National League Championship Series
Game 4: Brewers 4, Cardinals 3

The way this season has gone for the Cardinals, neither their fans nor the players expected anything to come easy.

On a night when a victory would have given St. Louis a commanding three-games-to-one lead in the best-of-seven series, their starting pitching failed to do enough to get a victory. Kyle Lohse could not protect a 2–0 lead and the Brewers claimed a 4–2 win, evening the series at two games each.

"We haven't done anything the easy way, so why start now?" Lohse said.

Solo home runs by Matt Holliday and Allen Craig staked Lohse to a two-run lead heading to the fourth inning, but it only took a four-batter span for the Brewers to tie the game. After a leadoff Nyjer Morgan double in the fifth followed by a groundout, Lohse was out of the game: he handed the ball to manager Tony La Russa as reliever Mitchell Boggs came in from the bullpen.

"Tony is not going to let you get too deep if it looks like you are in trouble," Lohse said. "That's the way he's been doing it. The bullpen has been doing a great job. I know that going in, and I've got to do a better job of keeping them off the board."

Boggs was greeted by an RBI single by Ryan Braun that gave the Brewers a lead they never relinquished.

This was the fourth time in as many starts in this series that the Cardinals' starting pitcher failed to last more than five innings. The four starters—Jaime Garcia, Edwin Jackson, Chris Carpenter and Lohse—lasted a combined 17 2/3 innings out of a possible 36 innings in the four starts. Combined they allowed 25 hits and 14 earned runs, which works out to be a 7.13 ERA.

As much as La Russa liked the makeup of the Cardinals' bullpen, trying to win a postseason series with that kind of performance out of the starting pitchers seemed nearly impossible.

Allen Craig makes perfect contact on his third-inning homer in Game 4.

"We had a chance to win today," La Russa said. "This is October. This is not the season where when this series is over you have to play for another 20 days or something. It's real simple. This is the end of the season for these starters, too, so they are probably not as strong. We have plenty of bullpen help.

"The better [the starters] pitch and the deeper they get in the game, then it's less outs for the bullpen. As hard as you can, as long as you can."

The loss did not dampen the spirit of the Cardinals, with the first-hand knowledge that they could come back from a deficit.

"I think people on the outside view this team as sort of a Cinderella story," Berkman said. "This is *not* a Cinderella story. We feel really good about where we're at."

Added infielder Nick Punto, "Maybe we weren't supposed to beat the Phillies, and we weren't supposed to catch the Braves. But we did. And now that we've advanced this far, I think it's silly for people to be suggesting that we're not supposed to advance again or win this series. We think we can win. That's what we're here to do." ●

Ryan Braun tried to break up the double play, but Rafael Furcal was able to make the turn and nab Prince Fielder after his fifth-inning ground ball.

Jason Motte

Hard-throwing former catcher keys Cards' late-season bullpen resurgence

Jason Motte is pretty scary when he comes walking in from the Cardinals' bullpen with opponents knowing he is going to throw a baseball at them at almost 100 miles per hour.

They would be even more afraid if they knew Motte sometimes can't see where the baseball is going.

Motte is nearsighted, and wears glasses when he is not pitching. He switches to contact lenses when he's on the mound, but sometimes his eyes get dry or the lenses fog up. On those occasions he has to squint to try to see the signals from catcher Yadier Molina.

"I'm glad he's on my team," Cardinals outfielder Matt Holliday said. "I'm not sure I want to go up there against a guy who can't see when he's throwing a ball 100 mph."

In truth, Motte was not clocked at 100 miles per hour during any of his four National League Championship Series appearances against the Brewers. He did throw several pitches at either 98 or 99 miles per hour, still fast enough for him to overpower the Milwaukee hitters.

In those four appearances, Motte—who did not pick up his first save in the regular season until Aug. 28—retired all 14 batters he faced, covering 4⅔ innings. He did not allow a hit or walk and struck out four, twice earning four-out saves.

When the Division Series is added to Motte's total, his performance is even more impressive. In seven appearances covering eight innings, Motte earned four saves, allowed just one hit, did not walk a batter, and struck out seven, retiring 24 of the 25 batters he faced, including the final 19 in a row.

It almost became a standing joke in St. Louis that manager Tony La Russa refused to label Motte as the team's closer, saying instead that he was the pitcher who got the last three outs when the Cardinals were ahead on that day.

The fact that Motte does not have that label does not concern him one bit. For a pitcher who worked anywhere between the third and 10th inning this year, he knows to be ready whenever the phone in the bullpen rings and the call is for him.

"My job is to go out there and try to get the guy out that I'm facing, and if I don't get him out, try to get the next guy out and to keep doing it until Tony comes and takes the ball away from me," Motte said. "That's the way I look at it."

The performance of Motte and his fellow relievers was one of the major keys to the Cardinals' victory over the Brewers. The bullpen actually had to record more outs in the six games than the starting pitchers, none of whom went more than five innings in a game.

"He throws hard, he throws strikes, and he gets guys out," said teammate Arthur Rhodes, who became a member of the St. Louis bullpen in August after being released by Texas. "He kept it calm and cool and he did it the right way. He's done that, and look at where we're at right now." ●

The charismatic Jason Motte celebrates after closing out a late-season game against the Mets. Finally breaking through as the Cardinals' closer, Motte made the most of his opportunity in 2011.

National League Championship Series
Game 5: Cardinals 7, Brewers 1

In the spring of 2006, the Cardinals were considering releasing Jason Motte from their minor-league organization. In three seasons, almost all in Class A or rookie ball, the catcher had not shown much of an ability to hit and most observers did not see any hope that the situation would improve.

There was one part of the 24-year-old Motte's game that the Cardinals did like, however. He had a great arm, and consistently threw out almost all of the runners who tried to steal against him.

What do you think, someone suggested, about trying to make him a pitcher?

"Before we gave him his release, we decided to put him on the mound and see what happened," said Mark DeJohn, now the Cardinals' field coordinator but five years ago, the man who became Motte-the-pitcher's first

manager in State College, Pennsylvania, in the New York-Penn League.

DeJohn was reminded again of the story of how far Motte has come in five years during Game 5. He sat at his home in Connecticut, watching on television as Motte closed out another victory for the Cardinals, this time bringing them within one win of a trip to the World Series.

Motte's second four-out save of the NL Championship Series completed a 7–1 win over the Brewers, putting the Cardinals ahead three games to two.

The Cardinals were ahead 5–1, but the Brewers had two runners on base with two outs in the eighth inning when manager Tony La Russa called for Motte to come out of the bullpen to face Rickie Weeks, with the potential tying run on deck. Motte needed just two pitches to get Weeks to ground out to third, ending the threat, and then retired all three batters in order in the ninth.

Yadier Molina celebrates on second base after his second-inning double in Game 5 drove in Lance Berkman and gave the Cardinals a 1–0 lead.

The outing extended Motte's string of dominance in this postseason. He became only the third pitcher in franchise history to record four saves in one postseason, joining Dennis Eckersley in 1996 and Adam Wainwright in 2006.

In the division series and the championship series combined, Motte had retired 21 of the 22 batters he faced, allowing only a single to the Phillies' Placido Polanco in Game 3 of the NLDS. Following that hit, he retired 16 batters in a row, including all 11 batters he faced in the NLCS.

Motte, a 19th-round draft choice in 2003 out of Iona College in New York, remembers getting the news that the organization wanted to see if he could become a pitcher—a position he had never played before at any level growing up.

"It was tough at first because I didn't really know how it was going to go," Motte said. "It was one of those things when they told me they were turning me into a pitcher, I knew I could be at home. I knew my time as a catcher was over."

Motte still remembers that shaky first outing on the mound. He was in Williamsport, Pennsylvania, and he admits he had no idea what he was doing.

"I had always been behind the plate," he said, "but I just went out there and told myself to give it everything I had to every batter, just like it would be my last. I had great coaches along the way. It's been a learning process and I'm still learning, because the guy at the plate is always making adjustments, too."

Motte's success was just part of the bigger story of the bullpen's performance in this series. Through Game 5, the team's starting pitchers recorded only two more outs than the relievers. On this night, La Russa summoned Dotel from the bullpen when starter Jamie Garcia was one out away from qualifying for the win. Dotel came in to face Ryan Braun, who was 17-for-36 in the postseason, and Dotel did what he has usually done against him in his career—he struck him out. This time made it eight strikeouts in 10 at-bats by Braun against Dotel.

That was the first of 13 outs the bullpen recorded in this game, the final four by Motte.

DeJohn and all of the others who have watched Motte's five-year journey to reach this point in his career have every confidence that if he is on the mound in the ninth inning, however, he will bring home the victory for the Cardinals.

"It's an unbelievable accomplishment, how far he's come," DeJohn said. "He never would have got out of A ball if he had stayed a catcher. He had a good attitude and he worked hard. It's wonderful to see him doing so well."

Jason Motte fires a pitch in the eighth inning of the Cardinals' decisive Game 5 win.

National League Championship Series

Game 6: Cardinals 12, Brewers 6

The night before Game 6, Jason Motte was having dinner with some of his teammates, watching the end of the final game of the AL Championship Series. He paid particular attention to Neftali Perez, the Texas closer, when he recorded the final out of the game.

"I was getting goose bumps sitting in the restaurant," Motte said. "I was thinking, *man, that must be an awesome feeling.*"

About 24 hours later, Motte knew what it felt like—and it was awesome.

Motte recorded the final three outs of the Cardinals' 12–6 win, which capped another terrific performance by the team's bullpen and secured the 18th NL pennant in franchise history.

A four-run first inning, highlighted by a three-run homer by home-town hero and NLCS MVP David Freese, sparked the Cardinals to a quick 5–1 lead, but the Brewers made it 5–4 with three runs in the second. That's when Tony La Russa began calling on his bullpen once again, and they kept the Brewers at bay while the offense added more insurance runs.

The bullpen finished the series getting 13 more outs than the starters and compiled a 1.88 ERA, holding the Brewers to a .155 batting average. It was the first time a team won a postseason series without having any of its starters go more than five innings in a game.

The Cardinals won by scoring first in every game of the series, becoming the first team in postseason history to be able to make that claim, and by scoring in 15 of the 27 innings they played in Miller Park, where the Brewers had the best home record in MLB in 2011.

The Cardinals won because they didn't quit back in August, when they were 10½ games behind the Braves in the wild-card race and they didn't

The celebration was on in Milwaukee as the Game 6 win catapulted the Cardinals to a World Series date with the Texas Rangers.

quit when they were three games back with five to play. They did not make it in until the final game of the regular season, but once they got there, they saw the opening they needed.

And St. Louis won because of the hometown kid, Freese, who was the first player acquired in a trade by John Mozeliak after he became the team's general manager in 2007. Freese was sitting in a Burger King in Los Angeles when he got the word, and at first he thought it was some of his friends playing a trick on him. It took him a while to believe it was true, that the Padres had traded him to the Cardinals for Jim Edmonds.

Four years later, he was on a temporary stage, accepting the MVP trophy after hitting .545 with three homers and nine RBI in the six games. "Not too many people get a chance to do this in their hometown," Freese said. "It's an unbelieving feeling."

That was exactly the phrase Motte used to describe getting the final out, knowing the Cardinals were headed to the World Series.

"Yadi throwing his hands out," Motte said as he recalled what happened after he struck out Mark Kotsay. "I don't remember much after that. Yadi hugging me, me hugging him, next thing you know we're on the ground and everyone on the team is standing over us."

That group included Dotel, who pulled the stuffed squirrel out of the pocket of his sweatshirt where it had been for the final few outs of the game. The squirrel was as wet from the champagne showers as were all of the Cardinals.

"I feel like this has been good luck, and I'm going to keep it all the way through," Dotel said.

Nobody was about to talk him out of that, either. ●

Octavio Dotel celebrates with the stuffed "rally squirrel" that became a mascot of the Cardinals' playoff run after real squirrels found their way onto the field in separate games of the NLDS.

The St. Louis Cardinals celebrate after their 12-6 win over the Milwaukee Brewers in Game 6 of the National League Championship Series advanced them to the World Series.